Worship: ir

Worship

In the Body of Christ

By Stephen Dailly

Worship: in the Body of Christ

First published in 2013
Revised with additional material in 2016

2nd edition:
©2020 Stephen Dailly
ISBN: 9781521580806

Imprint: Independently published

Contents

Worship 5
1. Why does God need our worship? 10
2. What is 'Worship'? 20
3. The Role of the Worship Leader 41
4. The Tabernacle 54
5. The Outer Court 68
6. The Sanctuary (the Holy Place) part 1 85
7. The Sanctuary (the Holy Place) part 2 106
8. Intimacy with God 120
10. Using the Bible, Songs and Testimony 158
11. Prayer 173
12. Spiritual Gifts 195
13. "The Anointing that Breaks the Yoke" 222
14. Worship and Mission 250
Bibliography 278

I can safely say, on the authority of all that is revealed in the Word of God, that any man or woman on this earth who is bored and turned off by worship is not ready for heaven.

A.W. Tozer

Worship

I was made to love you, I was made to find you
I was made just for you, made to adore you
I was made to love and be loved by you.

(Toby Mac)

Introduction

Worship is natural for humans. We were made to worship; made in the image of God. When God looks at each of us, he longs to see his image reflected in our lives; in our actions and in our attitudes. He reveals his love to us, and we answer with a loving response. That's the heart of worship.

This material grew out of an idea for a course for new worship leaders at Her Majesty's Prison Dovegate. Several of the men involved had only recently come to Christ and none were very confident musicians, so we spent some Tuesday afternoons learning songs and talking about worship. While the course itself turned out to be difficult to do for a number of reasons, the ideas behind it and the material were strong and form the basis of this book.

If we were to go back fifty years, nobody was a 'worship leader'. Churches had musicians, song-leaders, organists and pianists, maybe even a 'director of music'. The idea of a 'worship leader' is quite a new thing ... and that should make us cautious. The Bible says nothing about worship leaders. The church of Jesus Christ has been just fine for two thousand years without worship leaders, so why do we need them now?

Perhaps we don't.

It might be something to do with the emphasis we put on personality nowadays, on faces and on style. I think this could be dangerous, or at least distracting. In the end, worship comes down to how I respond to God, and when we're together in church, it's how we – the Body of Christ – respond to God. The identity or personality of the person at the front should not be relevant.

In the Old Testament, the pattern of worship was detailed, complicated and prescribed. A whole clan of people was given responsibility for serving God in worship and in religious ritual. These people – the Levites – were responsible for looking after the Tabernacle (the special Tent where the people met with God) and later the Temple, and for praise and worship. A section of them – the descendants of Aaron – were the priests, who made sacrifices on behalf of the people.

Worship in the New Testament is much simpler. Whereas in the Old Testament the Priests and Levites met with God on behalf of the whole community, in the New Testament we are all free to meet with him individually. When we meet together it's helpful if someone convenes the meeting and provides a setting within which we worship; it may be helpful for that person to prepare songs and lead the congregation in praise.

Perhaps 'convener' is a better term than worship leader.

The purpose of this book

It's refreshing to strip an activity such as worship right back to its principles and ask the basic questions: what is worship? Why should we worship? What is the purpose of corporate worship? What happens when we worship?

It's also refreshing, as I often find in prison ministry, to work with people who aren't 'cultural' Christians; who often don't have the language and vocabulary of the 'church'; who don't (wish to!) understand denominations and simply want to walk with God, experiencing his love and power in their lives.

> *I acknowledge that many churches have organisational structures where particular people are qualified or selected for particular roles; this material is written from a perspective where no such structures exist and where anyone could be invited to lead worship. I belong to a small Evangelical congregation in the Midlands where I lead worship sometimes; I've also participated in several evangelistic and other events as a worship leader.*

The purpose of this material is to give an overview of the relationships and dynamics involved in worship as we approach God, regardless of the specific context.

Whom is this book intended for?

I hope that anyone who wants to worship God should find something helpful, thought-provoking or challenging here. I have tried in each chapter to go back to the first principles of what we are doing and why; it's not my intention to push any denominational or sectarian line. I have written with those people in mind who find themselves, as I have, with the responsibility to lead people in worship.

I'd like to thank a few people without whose help and support this book would not have happened. The dozen or so men at HMP Dovegate who showed up when they could on Tuesday afternoons in the Autumn of 2012; Sandie Hicks and Don Williams the Free Church Chaplains, and Brian K. the chapel orderly for excellent conversations and coffee.

Versions of the Bible

Mostly I'm using the New King James Version of the Bible (NKJV), but from time to time I refer to other translations of Scripture.

> NKJV: The Holy Bible, New King James Version, copyright 1982 by Thomas Nelson, Inc.

> KJV: The King James (Authorised) Version, Crown Copyright.

> NLT: Holy Bible. New Living Translation, copyright 1996, 2004, 2007 by Tyndale House Foundation.

YLT: Young's Literal Translation, public domain.

NIV: Holy Bible, New International Version, NIV, copyright 1973, 1978, 1984, 2011 by Biblica.

NIRV: New International Readers' Version (NIRV), copyright 1996, 1998 by Biblica.

1. Why does God need our worship?

Many Spirit-filled authors have exhausted the thesaurus in order to describe God with the glory He deserves. His perfect holiness, by definition, assures us that our words can't contain Him. Isn't it a comfort to worship a God we cannot exaggerate?

(Francis Chan)

This is a very common question and just beneath it is a protest: I thought God gave us free will, so why do I have to worship him? In our culture, God is often depicted as a tyrant, dispensing arbitrary 'justice' like Blake's Ancient of Days, or sitting by impassively as poor people suffer. Sometimes he is seen as an irrelevant relic of antiquity or the object of 'fundamentalist' belief, driving young men and women to sacrifice themselves and kill others in the name of a medieval religion. Our modern understanding often struggles with the idea of God at all when science and technology seem to hold so many keys. How does the God – Yahweh – who gave commands to a nomadic tribe in the Sinai desert 3,500 years ago, have anything to say to us in the twenty-first century?

Another common question: Does God lack self-esteem and need constant affirmation? This is a kind of naïve response to some of the verses in the Bible that instruct us to worship God. If God is so powerful, why does he lay so much importance on us worshipping him? What could my worship possibly give him that he doesn't already have? Or, as Christina Rossetti asked with a different attitude, What can I give Him, poor as I am?

Both of these are responses to God at a human level; it is how we might react to a person who constantly craves attention: notice me! Notice me! But God isn't like that. Firstly, he is God; he is worthy of our worship and praise; secondly, he invites us into a relationship with him through worship. As we encounter God and begin to know him; as we allow him to show himself to us, he changes us.

To worship: To honour or revere as a holy thing; to adore with appropriate acts; to regard with extreme respect or devotion; to adore. (Shorter Oxford Dictionary)

Is God Worthy of Worship?

> *In the beginning God created the heavens and the earth.*
>
> *(Genesis 1: 1)*

This is a simple statement at the very beginning of the Bible that God created everything. 'The heavens and the earth' covers everything that exists; God is superior to all things, superior to us and therefore worthy of our respect, honour and worship.

> *The heavens declare the glory of God; and the firmament shows His handiwork.*
>
> *(Psalm 19: 1)*

We naturally assume that the Creation was made for our benefit; we try to interpret it in our terms. This is understandable because we don't have another frame of reference; just like the people centuries ago who thought that the earth was at the centre of the universe, we think that God created everything for us. But the heavens declare the glory of God puts them in their proper perspective – a point made powerfully by Louie Giglio in his DVD presentation *Indescribable*[1]. The more we discover about the vastness of the universe, the more we discover about the vastness of God. When the words of Psalm 19 were written, only a few thousand stars were visible to observers, now, of course, we know much more and new and more amazing things are discovered about the universe all the time. Far from making the statement invalid, new discoveries reinforce it. God is amazing: *Who is like You, glorious in holiness, fearful in praises, doing wonders?* (Exodus 15: 11).

The word 'handiwork' (in the older translations) almost appears casual, as if the universe is something that God has knocked off on a Saturday afternoon. I like it because it emphasises his role as Creator, engaging with the world of physical reality, rather than an invisible and ephemeral spirit-world. In Genesis 2 we see God planting a garden; when God became a man as Jesus, he worked as a carpenter. Handiwork.

> *Who has measured the waters in the hollow of*
> *His hand, measured heaven with a span and*
> *calculated the dust of the earth in a measure?*
> *Weighed the mountains in scales and the hills in*

> *a balance? ¹³ Who has directed the Spirit of
> the LORD, or as His counsellor has taught Him?*
>
> *(Isaiah 40: 12, 13)*

Our temptation always is to think of God in human terms; we naturally think he's a bit like us. Here Isaiah emphasises that God is transcendent. Oceans, sky, mountains and the 'dust of the earth'; these things are the context of our lives, they define our environment, but God is so far above these limits, so much bigger in scale that the seas are a mere handful to him; he can measure off the universe with a span of his fingers and weigh the mountains like a market trader.

He is also beyond us in wisdom: who has directed the Spirit of the LORD; or … taught Him? We don't understand. We catch glimpses, but it's as if 'the more we know the less we know we know.' God surpasses us in every sense; the whole of our life is incidental to him. He is worthy of worship.

> *You are worthy, O Lord, to receive glory and
> honour and power; for You created all things,
> and by Your will they exist and were created.*
>
> *(Revelation 4: 11)*

In the fourth chapter of Revelation, the glorified Jesus speaks to John, now advanced in years. Having received various messages for the church from the Spirit of God, John sees a door standing open in heaven and hears a voice like the sound of a trumpet telling him to 'Come up here'. God, in the person of Christ, is inviting John into

the secret of his presence and he sees in a kind of
metaphor what is going on in heaven – in the spiritual
realm – all the time. God is being worshipped and
praised by his creation. John had, and we have, the
opportunity to join in.

Not only is God great and mighty, but he's also
interested in us!

Our Response
Of course, God has no trouble believing in himself – but
we sometimes doubt him. When we worship, we are
reminded of important truths that we can sometimes
forget. As we've just seen, there are good reasons to
worship simply because of Who He Is.

But perhaps the most immediate reason for us to
worship God is our own testimony or faith story. Our
own experience of God – the knowledge that he has
intervened in our lives and saved us – will drive our
desire to worship and to maintain a close relationship
with him.

We worship God, not as a distant Creator who once
lit the fuse of the universe and then stood back to wait for
the Big Bang; nor as the LORD 'Yahweh' of the Old
Testament, who thundered from mountain tops and
spoke to the nations through his prophets, but in the
Lord Jesus Christ: Emmanuel – God with us.

Jesus

> *The Word became flesh and dwelt among us, and we beheld His glory, the glory as of the only begotten of the Father, full of grace and truth.*
>
> *(John 1: 14)*

Jesus is the Word of God. When God spoke in the Beginning, Jesus was present (see Colossians 1: 15-18 by Him all things were created…); he became flesh, in other words a human being. We can worship God from a distance as the Creator of the Universe, but he has inserted himself into the creation – made himself subject to the laws of nature – so that we can know him. As we get to know him, we begin to understand who he really is. We behold his glory! We can't look straight at God in his glory, but we can look at Jesus – the man who reveals God.

> *For it is the God who commanded light to shine out of darkness, who has shone in our hearts to give the light of the knowledge of the glory of God in the face of Jesus Christ.*
>
> *(2 Corinthians 4: 6)*

The creation story in Genesis 1 describes God shining into darkness and chaos and creating order and distinction, light and darkness, sea and land, day and night, etc. When we align ourselves with Jesus; as we focus on him, the same process takes place in us by the action of the Holy Spirit, and our attitudes, our values and our sense of ourselves changes. If we want to know God, we find him in Jesus Christ.

How do we do this? We look at the Gospels. What does Jesus say and do? What is his teaching? How does he relate to people? How does he relate to women; to the sick; to the children; to vulnerable people? We see the character of God in these things. How does Jesus relate to God (whom he always calls Father)?

This realisation of God shines into our lives like a light.

> *Let this mind be in you which was also in Christ Jesus, [6] who, being in the form of God, did not consider it robbery to be equal with God, [7] but made Himself of no reputation, taking the form of a bondservant, and coming in the likeness of men. [8] And being found in appearance as a man, He humbled Himself and became obedient to the point of death, even the death of the cross. [9] Therefore God also has highly exalted Him and given Him the name which is above every name, [10] that at the name of Jesus every knee should bow, of those in heaven, and of those on earth, and of those under the earth, [11] and that every tongue should confess that Jesus Christ is Lord, to the glory of God the Father.*
>
> *(Philippians 2: 5-11)*

Jesus is God. He was God in the beginning; he was God when he lived as a man on earth. He is God now, reigning in heaven with his Father. He will be God when he returns to earth as king to reign.

He did not consider it robbery to be equal with God. We like to strive for better things. The best position, the best reputation, the best paid job, the best guitar riff, the biggest home-grown onions. Jesus didn't do that. The NIV translation says that he didn't consider equality with God something to be grasped – it was his by right. Instead, he became a human being … he allowed himself to die … he allowed himself to be falsely accused and tortured to death as a criminal. This also reveals the attitude of God (the light of the knowledge of the glory of God): he is humble. He made himself of no reputation.

And because of this Jesus' Father intervened to restore his proper place. God has highly exalted him – has lifted him up – and made him higher and more powerful than anything else in the universe (see Romans 8: 38, 39). Jesus is Lord! We must worship him, and we shall. In fact, we can either do it now because we love him, or we'll have to in the end, anyway.

Summary

God is worthy of our praise and our worship because he created the universe in all its diverse, majestic beauty. It displays how amazingly powerful he is.

We worship him because he shows us that he has power over our lives, yet he cares about us. We see John being invited to peek into the court of heaven to see what goes on in the actual presence of God.

God entered the world and revealed himself in Jesus. Why? John 3: 16 – God so loved the world that he gave his … Son, that whoever believes in him should not die. As we look at Jesus, we see God clearly: we see what he does and what he's like.

We worship him because God – as Jesus – humbled himself. He made himself nothing. Far from standing by while the poor and vulnerable are hurt, he can sit beside the poorest, most hurting and injured person on earth and embrace him. He said: (Luke 18: 16 NLT) Let the children come to me. Don't stop them! For the Kingdom of God belongs to those who are like these children; he was (Isaiah 53: 3) – despised and rejected by men, a man of sorrows and acquainted with grief. Yet because of this he is now 'highly exalted'. Jesus is the name before which every knee must bow; the name by which we must be saved (Acts 4: 12).

We can worship him, not as a distant deity, but as a present, living person who is concerned for us and with us. We worship God as he reveals himself to us.

Discussion 1

What is 'worship'?

Why is God worthy of worship?

Give an example of a time of worship that you enjoyed or that you feel brought you into a closer relationship with God.

- Where was it?
- What happened?
- Who was participating?

Give an example of a worship time that left you cold or unmoved.

- What do you think went wrong?

Suggest some factors or 'ingredients' that would constitute a 'good' worship time?

In some churches these days, there is an emphasis on well-known and charismatic worship-leaders.

- Are there ways in which it is beneficial to have celebrity worship-leaders?
- Are there ways in which it is unhelpful?

2. What is 'Worship'?

So, worship is our response to God as he reveals himself to us.

God has created us; he has created everything around us. His grace saved us, gives us life and provides what we need from day to day and from moment to moment.

It is a fact that whether we believe in God or not, and whether or not we accept the sacrifice of Jesus Christ for our sins, we live our lives before him. However, as Christians, we are aware of God's presence with us and seek to spend time each day with him in prayer and reading the Scriptures. In that sense, everything we do could be called 'worship', and when we come together as the church, every part of that service is worship. It is our response – our service – to God. (That's why it's called a Service.)

Nowadays, there is a tendency to separate out the various parts of our response to God – the 'ministry', 'prayer' and 'worship' – from each other, to see them as separate.

'Jeff's doing the Ministry; Sue's doing the prayers; I'm leading worship.'

We sometimes say these things, but it's a mistake – it's a misunderstanding of what worship is. When we come together in Jesus' name, he is personally with us through the Holy Spirit and everything we do is worship.

This is very clear in churches that use liturgies.

Free-form or set structure

A liturgy[2] creates a detailed order for worship in which everything is included. In many churches, especially the more traditional ones, liturgy is the norm. In fact, this is where we get Christmas, Easter and Pentecost from. Churches that don't celebrate Christmas are sometimes regarded as a bit odd, but the reason we have these religious festivals is because they are part of a 'church calendar', the traditional rota of events and celebrations held throughout the year.

Liturgies typically determine certain prayers, songs and Bible readings for particular services, and particular parts of the service. For those of us more used to 'free-form' worship, this can sound restricting – stifling, even. On the other hand, for those brought up in Roman Catholic, Church of England, Methodist or Lutheran traditions, it can be very hard to think outside of these structures.

But even 'free' churches often have liturgies. If you think about it, if you work out the order of what you're going to do, that's a sort of liturgy – especially if you do the same thing again next week.

So, if worship is our response to how God reveals himself to us, is it best to write down an order of what we're going to do, or should we just be spontaneous?

Advantages of using liturgy

Connection with the past. Through the ages, Christians have tried to work out the best forms of words to use in worship. There is great wisdom and depth in many of the forms used in traditional churches, not only in liturgy but many old hymns contain a wealth of experience and teaching that isn't always matched in modern worship songs. Sometimes, using these old forms and songs can give us a sense that we share our Christian experience with all the men and women who have followed Jesus since Bible times – like the 'cloud of witnesses' mentioned in Hebrews 12: 1.

Prayers. Sometimes congregations can fall into the trap of all their prayers becoming focused on the needs of their particular group. Of course, we need to pray about those things, but we must also acknowledge that we are part of the wider Body of Christ. Having set prayers or set themes for prayers can help to get the balance right.

Some people find it very hard to pray aloud in public, and especially hard to lead others in prayer. It can be embarrassing to be tongue-tied, so having something written down can help. Written prayers may help us to capture our thoughts and express them in good ways.

Integrity of worship. In a liturgy, everything we do together as church is seen as part of the same 'act of worship' including singing, reading the Bible, praying and preaching. This is as it should be.

Disadvantages and dangers of using liturgy

Insincerity. We should respond naturally to God and not always need to have things written down for us. The closest person to me is my wife. I might take some time over writing her a poem to celebrate her birthday, but if I'm going to ask her if she wants a cup of tea or tell her that I love her, I probably shouldn't need to write those things down.

There are times when it's absolutely right to approach God with solemnity and great seriousness; he's God! But there are many times when he invites us to be completely open with him and times when he draws us into a place of intimacy. These cannot be scripted.

"Dead". When everyone relies on a book or service sheet for their worship, or where they are passively 'consuming' someone else's singing, music or preaching, they no longer have to rely on the Holy Spirit. They might find that they can only worship in this way. That would be wrong – Jesus is the only Mediator we need (1 Timothy 2: 5).

Some churches have separate services for those who prefer a traditional-style worship such as the old Prayer Book and those who prefer a more contemporary style. Somewhere they seem to have lost sight of what they're doing. Our worship together, as we'll discuss later, must be an expression of the Body of Christ serving and supporting one another.

Separation between 'priest' and 'people'. In some congregations, all the 'leading' is done by a few people for or on behalf of the rest of the church. This is not what the New Testament teaches about worship.

Spontaneity

Is it possible to worship 'spontaneously' in church, or will this end up as chaos?

I've been in many 'unscripted' meetings and often there is a powerful sense of God's presence – but not always. In chapter 12 we'll look at Paul's teaching to the Corinthian church on worship where he emphasises the need for order and clarity. When we meet together it's usually necessary for the service to be led by someone.

But this does not rule out spontaneity; there should always be the opportunity for open and unscripted periods in our meetings to ensure that everyone has the opportunity to participate actively.

Ex-tempore is a better term than 'spontaneous'; these are opportunities for God to speak among his people 'out of the moment'.

Worship is our response to God

God reveals himself to us in the Bible and in our personal experience. Our worship is our response to these things.

For some people, the essence of worship is personal devotion to God. When they come to church, they want only to meet with him and to exclude all distractions. We might come to the conclusion that this is the main thing; that the purpose of worship is to express our adoration to God and to pursue holiness. To others, the main purpose is to have fellowship with other Christians and to experience a shared journey of faith. We might conclude that worship is all about 'building the Body of Christ'.

There can be a tension between these things; between our personal need for devotion to God and our need to encourage one another, but if we carefully read and understand what the Bible says we should get the balance right.

> *[speak] to one another in psalms and hymns and spiritual songs, singing and making melody in your heart to the Lord...*
>
> *(Ephesians 5: 19)*
>
> *Let the word of Christ dwell in you richly in all wisdom, teaching and admonishing one another in psalms and hymns and spiritual songs, singing with grace in your hearts to the Lord.*
>
> *(Colossians 3: 16, my emphases)*

In worship, we are speaking and singing to the Lord and to each other.

Worship in Scripture

Bob Kauflin, in a passage about planning worship services writes[3]:

> *As we sit down and ponder what God wants to accomplish on Sunday we may start to feel very needy. People will be walking in confused, empty and bitter; facing financial worries, life-threatening illnesses and family struggles. We know that God is sovereign, wise and good, and*

> *that he cares for them. But they've forgotten that. We have God's word, four or five songs and thirty minutes to help them see that God is bigger than their problems and that Jesus Christ is a magnificent Savior. How can we arrange this time so people are best positioned to hear from God and receive his grace? What can we do to serve the church most effectively?*

Fortunately, our job is only to provide a way for God to work among his people. Our worship together should be directed in two ways: 'up' to God because he's worthy of praise and 'across' to our brothers and sisters, because the Holy Spirit will use us to encourage them and build them up. He knows our needs and longs to meet us there so that we can be whole to serve him more effectively; this is exactly what he wants to do. Let's look at two well-known Bible passages and see how he works.

Worship in Psalm 95
Psalm 95 gives a map of how we encounter God in worship.

> *Oh come, let us sing to the LORD! Let us shout joyfully to the Rock of our salvation.* [2] *Let us come before His presence with thanksgiving; let us shout joyfully to Him with psalms.* [3] *For the LORD is the great God, and the great King above all gods.* [4] *In His hand are the deep places of the earth; the heights of the hills are His also.* [5] *The sea is His, for He made it; and His hands formed the dry land.*

(Psalm 95: 1-5)

The Psalm starts with an invitation to the people to come and praise God: *Come, let us sing to the LORD!* This is something that everyone can do, and all can participate in. The writer starts off with a general invitation and breaks it down into specifics.

He is the rock of our salvation. God in the Old Testament sometimes refers to himself as a rock; a rock that's steady, secure and won't be either blown away by the wind or washed away by floods. We must come with thanksgiving, reminding one another that God is our provider and the source of everything we have. Is there something in particular that you are thankful for? In any case be thankful. We should shout *joyfully* with psalms. For 'psalms' we can read 'songs of praise'.

Sometimes we don't feel like shouting joyfully – in those cases we need to do it in obedience and allow the Holy Spirit to work. Often, we find that singing praise is a therapeutic activity.

Why should we do these things? *For the LORD is the great God, and the great King above all gods* (v.3). He is the supreme authority in the universe and therefore he deserves our praise. If we're feeling harassed by our circumstances or by individuals or organisations, God is bigger than they are, and we belong to him – so we can take courage and confidence in that.

In His hand are the deep places of the earth; the heights of the hills are His also (v.4) wherever we are, God is sovereign. Not only does he reign now, but he made the world and everything in it in the first place. Unemployed people; people in debt; sick people; people in bereavement, hospitals, prisons, psychiatric units and semi-detached houses can know that in their circumstances, whatever they are, God is sovereign and worthy to be praised. He is in the deep places of the earth – the heights are his also. Been there? You know it's true!

The sea is His, for He made it; and His hands formed the dry land (v.5). This sentence follows on from the previous one: deep places of the earth, heights, and now the sea. But I'd like to link it back to Genesis:

> *Then God said, "Let the waters under the heavens be gathered together into one place, and let the dry land appear"; and it was so. [10] And God called the dry land Earth, and the gathering together of the waters He called Seas. And God saw that it was good.*
>
> *(Genesis 1: 9, 10)*

After the initial creation, the earth – for reasons that are not obvious – finds itself in chaos: it was formless, empty and dark. God sets about creating order, and here in verses 9 and 10 he separates the land from the sea. We should praise God and worship him because he takes the empty, meaningless mess that life can be and creates order out of it. He gives it meaning, purpose and beauty – he makes it "good".

So, the beginning of Psalm 95 invites us to sing praise to God because we all have good reason to, but mostly because he's worthy of it: the great king above all gods.

> *Oh come, let us worship and bow down; let us kneel before the LORD our Maker.* [7] *For He is our God, and we are the people of His pasture, and the sheep of His hand.*

(Psalm 95: 6, 7a)

In this section, the Psalmist brings us to a more intimate place of worship. We have started with a recap of what God has done and a declaration of praise, but now we come quietly to present ourselves before him.

Oh come, let us worship and bow down (v.6): making a statement of praise that God is good, is only one thing; for our worship to affect us seriously and for it to move him, we must be engaged at a deeper level.

Some people actually bow down when they pray, showing in their bodily posture what their attitude is in their heart; others don't often do this. The important thing is that we bow in our hearts. This requires a basic change in our attitude. We will listen to what God is going to say to us, we will look within ourselves and allow the Holy Spirit to work in our lives.

For He is our God, and we are the people of His pasture, and the sheep of His hand (v.7a). God cares for us. He wants to nurture and feed us like a shepherd looking after his sheep; he wants to teach us and build us up like a good teacher. As we come before him in worship, we open ourselves to his voice. He wants us to turn away from our mess and to seek his face; he wants us to read his Word in the Bible and understand his will; he wants us to care for one-another and to grow together in fellowship.

> *Today, if you will hear His voice: [8] "Do not harden your hearts, as in the rebellion, as in the day of trial in the wilderness, [9] when your fathers tested Me; they tried Me, though they saw My work. [10] For forty years I was grieved with that generation, and said, 'It is a people who go astray in their hearts, and they do not know My ways.' [11] So I swore in My wrath, 'They shall not enter My rest.'"*
>
> *(Psalm 95: 7b-11)*

This is really the crux of the matter – the 'heart of worship'. When we have acknowledged God as sovereign and given him thanks and praise for what he has done in general and for ourselves in particular, and after we have bowed ourselves in our minds and hearts before him, we must expect him to speak to us. What he says will probably be quite individual to us; what we hear in church on a Sunday morning will usually tie in with what the Holy Spirit has been saying to us all week if we've been listening. Sometimes he will speak to the whole church together.

The last section of Psalm 95 gives us a kind of general-purpose sermon outline. This is the kind of thing that God, the Good Shepherd, says to his people. It refers to the period, from Exodus through to Deuteronomy, where God – Yahweh – is leading the people of Israel through the wilderness and teaching them. It took them forty years because when they had the opportunity to take hold of the land that God had promised them, they let it slip away through fear and doubt. During those forty years, a whole generation was lost. So, God says: *Today, if you will hear His voice: Do not harden your hearts…* (vv.7,8).

If I can hear his voice today – as I'm reading these words, as I'm entering worship, as I'm listening to the preacher – I must not harden my heart.

It's easy to have a hard heart. Particularly, I think, for people who have been Christians for many years, who are 'generational' or 'cultural' Christians. We can get very familiar with the words of Scripture; they can become stale to us; almost whatever anyone says, we've heard it before. When a young preacher stands up in church to speak, full of the revelation that God has given him, there might be a sense of 'teaching grandma to suck eggs'; his words, given out of passion for God can fall on deaf ears. It can be devastating for him. We might commend him for his diligence and faithfulness, we might be quite complimentary, but we are unlikely to be moved by what God has said because he's a familiar face and he's speaking words we've heard before. Jesus faced the same problem (Mark 2: 6, 7).

Brothers and sisters, this is very important. Today, God is speaking to us. He is addressing you and me. He might not be thundering from a mountaintop in Israel or crying out with the voice of Elijah, but he is speaking nonetheless. He speaks directly into my life and to yours, and sometimes – perhaps often – we are too thick in the ear and too hard of heart to hear it. It is the tragedy of the Western Church. God gives us a word here in Psalm 95 (and repeats it in Hebrews 3 and 4): he says, if you can hear God speaking to you today, *do not harden your heart*.

Most of the rest of that passage develops the scene of the people in the desert, wrestling with God for forty years. The last words are a warning to us as they were to them: the people go astray and cling to their ignorance, so *I swore in My wrath, They shall not enter My rest* (v.11). The whole generation of those who missed the promised died out in that forty years; their children inherited it. We are in danger of the same thing every time we harden our hearts to what God is saying.

The heart of worship (I reiterate) is that God speaks to his people and that he gives us an opportunity to respond to him.

Worship in Isaiah 6: 1-9

This is one of the most famous passages in the Bible. In a vision, the prophet Isaiah sees himself in the presence of God, in the Most Holy Place. While this passage is very different from Psalm 95, they can both teach us about worship in the presence of God. In his vision, Isaiah is transported suddenly into the presence of God:

> *In the year that King Uzziah died, I saw the LORD sitting on a throne, high and lifted up, and*

> *the train of His robe filled the temple. ² Above it stood seraphim; each one had six wings: with two he covered his face, with two he covered his feet, and with two he flew. ³ And one cried to another and said: "Holy, holy, holy is the LORD of hosts; the whole earth is full of His glory!" ⁴ And the posts of the door were shaken by the voice of him who cried out, and the house was filled with smoke.*

(Isaiah 6: 1-4)

In this case, unlike in the previous example, Isaiah doesn't get to sing the praises of God out loud, instead he is plunged suddenly into the 'inside' of the presence of God – he struggles to describe what he sees.

This happens 'in the year that King Uzziah died': this is significant. King Uzziah overstepped his authority as king and did something that only a priest was supposed to do. In 2 Chronicles 26: 19-21 he went into the Holy Place of the Temple and burned incense on the Incense Altar. This might sound like a minor thing, but previously the sons of Aaron had been killed outright for doing something similar (in Leviticus 10). It seems that prophetic visions had been withheld from Isaiah until the time of Uzziah's death. Now, dramatically, his vision returns, and he finds himself in the presence of Yahweh, the LORD.

He is high and lifted up, and the train of His robe filled the temple (v.1). Imagine a bride on her wedding day: a royal bride: the Duchess of Cambridge had a fairly impressive train to her wedding dress – her sister carried it into the Abbey. If the length of the train is a very rough indicator of 'majesty', her late mother-in-law, Diana, outclassed her. But these are only a bit majestic. The LORD'S train *filled the temple*. It was *everywhere*. Isaiah's telling us how majestic he is: his glory doesn't just fill the aisle, it fills the entire building. And not only that; *above it stood seraphim*. We don't really know what 'seraphim' are – in fact this is the only time they're mentioned as such in the whole Bible; the word means 'burning-ones': they are angelic beings who cover and surround the presence of God.

So, God is high and majestic, and screened by almost indescribable fiery winged creatures. They cover their feet and their faces with their wings: why? Because their feet might touch the earth and be contaminated by something unholy, and because God is too majestic and holy for even the holiest and most formidable of his creatures to look at.

But – amazingly – Isaiah *can* look at him. Isaiah is made in the image of God – and so are we.

And one [seraph] cried to another and said: "Holy, holy, holy is the LORD of hosts; the whole earth is full of His glory!" (v.4). There is constant sound; the sound of beating wings and this constant shouting out. In the Hebrew language if a word is repeated it works as emphasis. Ben Nevis is big; Mont Blanc is big, big; Everest is big, big, big. Yahweh is holy, holy, holy: words cannot properly express how holy he is. Think of the Temple as in some way representing the whole world, or maybe the universe – the decorations on the inside of the Temple illustrated this. The image is of Yahweh's glory filling the whole of creation, just as we saw in the last chapter: Psalm 19: 1: The heavens declare the glory of God; and the firmament shows His handiwork. The whole earth is full of his glory.

But for Isaiah, he sees this, he witnesses it, but it almost passes above his head.

> *So I said: "Woe is me, for I am undone! Because I am a man of unclean lips, and I dwell in the midst of a people of unclean lips; for my eyes have seen the King, the LORD of hosts."*
>
> (Isaiah 6: 5)

Isaiah is aware of his sin – his unclean lips. This is not a man given to profane language – he's one of God's prophets. But he's aware that everything he says is contaminated by his human mind, and even if the words themselves are good they're coming from him – a flawed and fragile man. He's not holy and he is incapable of speaking holiness. The knowledge breaks his heart: I am undone. At that moment, the righteousness and holiness of God cuts him apart:

> *For the word of God is living and powerful, and sharper than any two-edged sword, piercing even to the division of soul and spirit, and of joints and marrow, and is a discerner of the thoughts and intents of the heart.*
>
> (Hebrews 4: 12)

This is a turning point in Isaiah's ministry. God will rebuild him, but first this realisation of the holiness of God set against his own uncleanness and the sinful people he lives among has to dismantle him completely.

For us, the experience of worship must echo this. We are coming into the presence of the living God, the Creator and Lord of the entire universe and this is not something we can do lightly. As we look on him, we will only see our utter hopelessness. Like Isaiah, we will be taken apart by the Word of God.

> *Then one of the seraphim flew to me, having in his hand a live coal which he had taken with the tongs from the altar. [7] And he touched my mouth with it, and said:*
>
> *"Behold, this has touched your lips; your iniquity is taken away, and your sin purged."*
>
> *(Isaiah 6: 6, 7)*

For Isaiah, one of the seraphim touches his lips with a coal from the altar, purging the sin from his lips. God often appears as fire (*like a refiner's fire* – Malachi 3: 2) because his Spirit cleanses and burns away anything that is not holy (see 1 Corinthians 3: 9-15). We must go through the same process of realisation as Isaiah as we come before God, but we don't need a coal to cleanse our lips. Jesus himself has taken our sin, so at the same time as realising the fact that we are sinful and can't be in the presence of God, we are also aware of the dreadful price that was paid by Jesus to make it possible.

> *He was wounded for our transgressions, He was bruised for our iniquities; the chastisement for our peace was upon Him ...*

(Isaiah 53: 5)

The well-known song by Gerrit Gustafson says:

> *Only by grace can we enter,*
> *Only by grace can we stand;*
> *Not by our human endeavour,*
> *But by the blood of the Lamb.*

Although Yahweh in this vision is high and lifted up and seen as the Lord of the universe, we understand that Isaiah has been brought there by invitation. He's not appearing before God for judgement, and although the holiness of God cuts him to the core, it doesn't destroy him.

> *Also I heard the voice of the* LORD, *saying: "Whom shall I send, and who will go for Us?"*
>
> *Then I said, "Here am I! Send me."*
>
> *⁹ And He said, "Go ..."*

(Isaiah 6: 8, 9)

These verses are parallel to the third section of Psalm 95 in that God is looking for an open-hearted response from us. There God said, *Today ... do not harden your hearts*; here, he asks two specific questions: *Whom shall I send?* In other words, he's going to give an instruction, and *Who will go for Us?* He's looking for someone willing to serve. This is an invitation into a partnership or 'joint enterprise'; a meeting of two compatible hearts. There is work to be done and Isaiah is eager to do it (now that he's been cleansed – he was no good before). Along with Isaiah, God invites us to be his partners in the work of redeeming the world.

The essence of worship

Worship brings us from wherever we were into alignment with God's will so that we can respond when he speaks to us; so that we can become partners with him. In a parallel passage at the end of Matthew's gospel, Jesus speaks to his disciples before he returns to his Father.

> *Then the eleven disciples went away into Galilee, to the mountain which Jesus had appointed for them. [17] When they saw Him, they worshipped Him; but some doubted.*
>
> *[18] And Jesus came and spoke to them, saying, "All authority has been given to Me in heaven and on earth. [19] Go therefore ..."*
>
> *(Matthew 28: 16-19)*

The risen Jesus had invited the eleven apostles to meet him on a mountain, where they worshipped him. The scene is undoubtedly very different from Isaiah's vision, with an absence of smoke and seraphim, but the same relationships are there. Yahweh in the vision is the

Lord of the Universe; Jesus here standing with his friends on a mountain declares: *All authority has been given to Me.* Jesus is the same as Yahweh, and when he says I am, it has the same power.

Like Yahweh, Jesus gives his authority to his disciples: *Go therefore ...*

When we come to worship, we are coming to meet with God. This is not a small thing, nor is it something that should be made into a routine. We come at his invitation: *Into Your presence You draw us*; we meet him on the 'mountain he has appointed for us' and he commissions us for service.

These are the foundations of worship. We come with praise and adoration, celebrating the amazing truths about God; he draws us closer and we come with open hearts to speak with him and hear his voice. Finally, he speaks to us as individuals and as a group and his Word transforms us.

Of course, God doesn't always send us out on some prophetic mission; he might just breathe our name as he did to Mary Magdalene in John 20, and that will be enough, but we cannot come into the presence of God and leave without being profoundly touched. We must expect to be changed – to be dismantled and reassembled – and to respond in some way.

If we leave our Sunday morning service the same way we enter it, we have missed the point; we have missed God's appointment.

Discussion 2

How does the God of the Old Testament, have anything to say to us in the twenty-first century?

What, if anything, does my worship give God that he doesn't already have?

In what ways do we commonly think of God in human terms?

- How can we move beyond this in worship?

Look at the 'hymn' sections in Revelation 4 and 5.

- Can you find words of your own to express the majesty and glory of God?
- In what way have you encountered the glory of God?

When you think of your own interaction with God, what words or phrases spring to mind?

> (If you would prefer to express yourself in a different medium, for example by drawing a picture or through music, that is fine.)

How do you perceive God?

What do you strive for?

3. The Role of the Worship Leader

Oh, Worship the LORD in the beauty of holiness.

(1 Chronicles 16: 29)

Meeting together

Our worship together is the highlight of the Christian's week. Maybe some of us will have met up in between times, but our worship service is different; we come to share in fellowship together and to meet with God our saviour. As he speaks to us, we respond to him.

And the pinnacle of that worship service is the preaching of the word. We expect to hear God speak; we expect to be changed; to be transformed and to have our minds renewed.

As we saw in the previous chapter, people arrive at a service in all sorts of conditions. One person might be facing difficulties, another may feel ill, another may be stressed; yet another may be suffering from depression or may have fallen again to a sin that they just can't beat. The God who loves us will meet these needs, just as Jesus in the gospels met the needs of those he ministered to. But our needs cannot become the focus of our worship time together – we don't come primarily to seek a solution to our problems or therapy for our hurts, we come to worship God and to hear what he has to say. In his compassion, he will meet our needs anyway.

The role of the worship leader, under the guidance of the Holy Spirit, is to gather all these wandering hearts and minds together and help them to participate in the meal that God has laid on.

Can you lead us in a song?
Sometimes we might be privileged to lead the whole service and introduce the preacher. Sometimes we might have ten or fifteen minutes, or we might only be asked to lead one song. In each case we have the opportunity to change the focus of the room and fix it onto Jesus.

The qualities of a worship leader

In 1 Timothy 3: 1-13 Paul writes to Timothy, a young church leader, about the qualities needed by *bishops* and *deacons*. In New Testament times, the 'bishops' were the leaders of the church and 'deacons' were people with practical responsibilities in the congregation. For us, a *bishop* might be the minister or senior pastor; a *deacon* could be anyone from the person who makes the coffee to the guy on the sound-desk. By this definition, the worship team are certainly *deacons*. The origin of the deacons appears to be in Acts 6: 1-7 where seven Spirit-filled men were selected to *serve tables*. It was important then that people were served by Spiritual people; the same is true now.

It may be that the worship leader is a leader or pastor in the church, maybe not, but in any case, leading a congregation in worship is itself a pastoral responsibility because it involves helping others to meet with God. It must be taken seriously; it's something that grows out of a mature walk with God.

Let's look in detail at Paul's specifications in 1 Timothy 3 for service in the church:

[Deacons should be] reverent (v.8). 'Reverent' means worshipful or respectful to God (and has nothing to do with collars). In order to worship God correctly, we must know Jesus Christ as our saviour and be filled with the Holy Spirit. This is the starting point of our spiritual conversation. Our attitude must be Christ-like; we should want to worship God more than anything else; in fact, we will see whatever we do as an aspect of worship. When we worship in song or with an instrument it will be a natural overflow of what's going on inside us.

Blameless (v.2, v.10). We must demonstrate Christ in our conduct not only on Sunday but on every other day of the week also. We must live worthily of the name of Jesus (Colossians 1: 10) because people will judge him by the way we live. Many people say that they don't go to church because they think Christians are hypocrites. This is likely to be untrue and is certainly unfair, but it is a common perception. We must strive to live selflessly and to demonstrate his love. Paul says *[bishops] must have a good testimony among those who are outside* (v.13). Romans 12: 9 – *Let love be without hypocrisy.*

The husband of one wife (v.2; v.12). (This appears in a list with temperate, sober-minded and hospitable.) This sounds an unlikely thing to say, but Paul lists it twice in these few verses – so he obviously thinks it's important.

While our marital status in itself will not affect our ability to worship or to lead others (I'm sure that unmarried people make perfectly acceptable leaders – Paul himself was unmarried), Paul is speaking about living in a moderate and stable way where what happens on Sunday morning reflects what goes on for the rest of the week. In Bible times, the church was based on household units and a stable marital relationship was at the heart of that, in fact it modelled the relationship between Christ and the Church (Ephesians 5: 22-33). Churches today have become organisations and have lost touch with their roots in the family unit. But at the centre of the Body of Christ is a loving relationship, firstly with him and also with each other. We need to recapture the 'household' aspect of church life based on family units.

At first sight, this can seem alienating to people in our fragmented society who are not part of a family group. What about singles? Divorcees? What about people with different sexual orientation? These are certainly issues that need to be addressed, but it is hard to project consistent love and compassion except through stable homes and households where hurting people can be esteemed and valued. This is why we must be *hospitable*.

Not a novice (v.6). We can't ask or expect new Christians to occupy responsible positions in the church straight away. They won't have sufficient Spiritual maturity to understand what is required of them or a deep enough understanding of the Word; they will still think in a 'worldly' way.

Able to teach (v.2). We can infer several things from this. As leaders in worship, we must be able to communicate with the congregation and with the leadership of the church; if there's a worship band, there will need to be good communication within that too.

We must be *Bible-focused* and have a secure grasp of theology and good doctrine in order to know what we believe, apply it to our lives and communicate it to others. When we introduce a song, for example, we might want to explain its significance, what God is saying through it and how it fits into the service.

Theology is what we understand about God and our relationship with him; *doctrine* is what is taught. Songs express these things, but sometimes they don't do it clearly or accurately. However, over time the songs and words used in worship will form a large part of the congregation's spiritual language – how they think and speak about God – so it's important that the songs and other resources we use have good Biblical theology, and that people grow in their understanding of God by singing them.

Not quarrelsome, not covetous (v.3). Any position of leadership is bound to attract criticism and probably attack. Playing in a worship band is one of the biggest trials of grace and patience I know! There is no room for people's egos in worshipping God; yet we all have them; we all want to assert ourselves and we all have opinions about how things should be done.

Relationships within worship teams are critical; teams must worship together before they get to 'lead' anyone. It's completely impossible to worship God the way he wants if there are disagreements and personal tussles going on among the team – these things have to be rapidly resolved. Several helpful books and resources are available on this subject[4].

I will go further and say that worship leaders in particular must be humble. This is a Christ-like attribute. When I stand and worship as part of the congregation, I don't want my attention drawn to the person leading. I want to be able to focus on Christ. Performance is the enemy of worship.

When I first started leading at my home Church, I didn't like to use the stage, instead I placed myself to one side where I would be inconspicuous. My belief was (and still is) that the leader should be transparent; anything of me that is seen is probably blocking something of God. In fact, this didn't work well in practice. If you're teaching people a new song, they have to see your face; if you're speaking to people, to be honest, it's quite rude not to look at them. So "humbly" I had to stand at the front.

Another problem for me is the paraphernalia that often seems to come with making music nowadays. It makes me uncomfortable; there's a music stand, microphone stand, stomp box, monitor speaker, maybe a video monitor and all the cables – a lot of stuff. And that's just me: if there's a band, multiply it by five, plus a bulky keyboard and drum-kit. And there's probably a stage too. All this gets between us and the people we're serving and forms a physical – or at least a visual – barrier, which is unhelpful.

The Body of Christ

> *We, being many, are one body in Christ.*
>
> *(Romans 12: 5)*

We need to understand two relationships: the vertical relationship between us and God, and the horizontal relationship – the 'fellowship' – between us as brothers and sisters. Both are important; we can't have the one without the other.

> *For I say, through the grace given to me, to everyone who is among you, not to think of himself more highly than he ought to think, but to think soberly, as God has dealt to each one a measure of faith. [4] For as we have many members in one body, but all the members do not have the same function, [5] so we, being many, are one body in Christ, and individually members of one another.*
>
> *(Romans 12: 3-5)*

Paul says, (using similar words as to Timothy) that we should think soberly, as God has dealt to each one the measure of faith (v.3). This isn't to do with not drinking, but about being sensible. At the beginning of chapter 12, Paul says:

> *I beseech you therefore, brethren, by the mercies of God, that you present your bodies a living sacrifice, holy, acceptable to God, which is your reasonable service.*
>
> *(Romans 12: 1)*

Presenting ourselves to God is reasonable, and when he says that we should think soberly it's the same thing. The more we understand of God (our theology and doctrine) the more reasonable or sober our thoughts will be. I've observed two opposite tendencies among some of the Christians I know. One group will say that they are sinners, saved by grace, and that the Holy Spirit is working in their lives to make them like Christ. The other group will say that they are saints; that they are made perfect in Christ and that the blood of Jesus Christ has cleansed them from every sin.

Neither of them is wrong: it's a question of perspective. Do we define ourselves by our starting position as sinners or our finishing point as people of God? Paul called the early Christians saints, yet he was conscious of the evil that was present with him (Romans 7: 21). Both of these groups see themselves in relation to 1 John 1 – *if we say we have no sin we deceive ourselves* (v.6) *but the blood of Jesus Christ cleanses us from all sin* (v.5) – both have come to Jesus and received cleansing.

Either way, we are to view ourselves as *God has [given us] the measure of faith*. What we believe about God and our relationship with him comes from what the Holy Spirit has shown us through our reading of the Bible, through good teaching and it will be confirmed through our experience. At first, we have a tiny circle of faith, a pinpoint of light, surrounded by a dark sea of doubt.

As we grow, the circle of our faith increases, and the doubt recedes. But it never goes away completely because God often calls us to live on the boundary where faith and doubt meet. As my faith increases, so my relationship with God deepens. This is what thinking soberly means.

For ... we have many members in one body (v.4). We will discuss the Body of Christ in much more detail later on. In this book, I use the term Body of Christ to mean the whole church, all the people of God, regardless of divisions and denominations.

So, we, being many, are one body in Christ (v.5). All of us are different – we have different gifts and abilities that God has given to us – yet we are united in Christ. He has saved us all from our sin, we've all made the same journey through Christ, and he lives in us by the Holy Spirit – we have a common testimony. *We are also members of one another* (v.6); we are affected by how other people are doing. If I'm running and stub my toe, my whole body will slow down; it might even flinch involuntarily because of the pain. The Body of Christ is like that: if the worship leader's having a bad day, people may miss the full power of what God is saying.

Verses 6-8 mention Spiritual gifts. These are not natural talents or abilities, but supernatural gifts that the Holy Spirit gives us. In Ephesians 4 Paul explains what they are for.

> *And He Himself gave some to be apostles, some prophets, some evangelists, and some pastors and teachers, [12] for the equipping of the saints for the work of ministry, for the edifying of the body of Christ, [13] till we all come to the unity of the faith and of the knowledge of the Son of God, to a perfect man, to the measure of the stature of the fulness of Christ.*
>
> *(Ephesians 4: 11- 13)*

In the Body of Christ, all our relationships are Spiritual – they grow out of who we are in Christ. The Holy Spirit works to help us function together and support one another; his purpose is to bring us to the ... *fulness of Christ* (v.13). Everything that Jesus was we will be; everything that he did we will do; not all of us individually but together as a Body.

> *[God] put all things under [Jesus'] feet, and gave Him to be head over all things to the church, [23] which is His body, the fulness of Him who fills all in all.*
>
> *(Ephesians 1: 22, 23)*

This is why in order to get to the fulness of Christ we need to be unified in our faith and to know the Son of God – Jesus.

So, when we're leading worship the Body of Christ is being built together as a whole; we are being strengthened by the Holy Spirit, who will speak to us through the Spiritual gifts that he gives. We must be open and sensitive to what God is doing among his people.

It is also important for Christians from different churches to meet together to worship from time to time. It strengthens our understanding of the unity of our faith, the fact that – even though we might disagree about certain things – it is Christ who has called us all into his Body.

> *Christ has no body but yours,*
> *No hands, no feet on earth but yours,*
> *Yours are the eyes with which he looks*
> *Compassion on this world...*
>
> *(Teresa of Avila)*

So, the role of the worship leader is to be a channel – a drain-pipe, as it were – for the Holy Spirit to flow into the assembled group. He or she should lead invisibly so that Christ is seen, and his word is heard. The outcome of this is that the Body of Christ will be strengthened and built up as we spend time in the presence of Jesus.

This is not just an occasional job. Like every other ministry in the church it is a vocation – something to which we are called. Our actions, our attitudes and words, every aspect of our lives, should be consistent with serving in the presence of God.

Discussion 3

Project: Find as many songs and hymns as you can on the subject of 'The Cross'.

- What is the oldest one you can find?
- What is the newest?
- Do these two songs treat the subject in a similar way or are there differences?

How important is 'personal preference' in worship?

- In selecting a church to attend.
- In selecting hymns or songs to sing.
- In establishing an 'order of service'.

I often use Psalm 95 as a guide to planning worship services. As you read the psalms and study the scriptures, it will be helpful for you to develop your own scriptural model.

One of the aims of leading worship is to bring the congregation to the point where they are open and responsive to what God is saying.

- How do we 'harden our hearts'?

Reflection: In this chapter we have looked at three movements in worship:

- declaring God's praise,
- drawing close and
- responding to God's voice.

Find suitable words or phrases to help you focus on each of these movements.

Worship: in the Body of Christ

4. The Tabernacle

Immanuel... God with us

(Matthew 1: 23)

*But Christ came as High Priest of the good
things to come, with the greater and more perfect
tabernacle not made with hands, ... with His
own blood He entered the Most Holy Place once
for all, having obtained eternal redemption.*

(Hebrews 9: 11, 12)

*Immortal, invisible, God only wise,
In light inaccessible hid from our eyes,
Most blessed, most glorious, the Ancient of Days,
Almighty, victorious, thy great Name we praise.*

(Walter Chalmers Smith, 1824-1908)

'Tabernacle' is a very old word used to mean a temporary meeting place like a tent or a shed; its origin is the same as 'tavern', also a place where people meet. In the Bible, the Tabernacle was the designated place where God agreed to meet with Moses and the Israelites, a sort of mobile temple.

When the Israelite people came out of Egypt with Moses and lived in the desert, God told them to make a big tent in the middle of their camp where the priests could meet with him and where he would actually live. In the next few chapters, I'm going to use the idea of the Tabernacle to describe some aspects of worship, but first we need to look at it closely in order to understand how it worked.

It seems odd to think that God should choose to live on top of a wooden box, and even odder to think that this should demonstrate his holiness. In fact, it teaches us a lot about holiness and what God is like.

Holiness

Holiness is not a word we use very much nowadays – and dictionaries don't really help us to understand it. It's a word that has always been associated with religion and with things that are mysterious, weird and possibly threatening.

God is holy. In Chapter 2 we saw in Isaiah 6 that the seraphim cried 'holy, holy, holy' to Yahweh, and that this showed that he was *most holy*. Holiness isn't something that God does or says; it is something fundamental about him. Holiness is God's nature.

The first time the word appears in the Bible is in Exodus 3 where Moses encounters God in the burning bush and where God reveals his name – Yahweh – to him.

> *Then He said, "Do not draw near this place. Take your sandals off your feet, for the place where you stand is holy ground." [6] Moreover He said, "I am the God of your father—the God of Abraham, the God of Isaac, and the God of Jacob." And Moses hid his face, for he was afraid to look upon God.*

(Exodus 3: 5, 6)

Holiness shows God's purity. The seraphim in Isaiah 6 covered their feet and their faces; here Moses has to take his sandals off, and he covers his face when he understands who God is. God is so pure that nothing earthly or imperfect can be in his presence – we must be invited into the presence of God, like Isaiah. God called to Moses out of the bush; the voice said, 'Come up here' to John in Revelation 4.

> *Oh, worship the LORD in the beauty of holiness!*
> *Tremble before Him, all the earth.*

(Psalm 96: 9)

Holiness also signifies God's majestic beauty. When he is worshipped and his power is displayed, the whole earth must pay attention. We've seen how God created the universe to display his glory, and as we look at Creation; the unimaginable size of the galaxies and the distances involved in astronomy; the intricacy in the structure of atoms and the complexity of DNA; we see an aspect of God's holiness. No one else could do things like that.

Both of these ideas lead up to the fact that God is not like us. He is very different. The word in Hebrew that we translate as 'holy' means separated or apart.

> *For I am God, and not man, the Holy One in*
> *your midst …*

(Hosea 11: 9)

He is God and not man; he is absolutely pure, righteous, magnificent, awesome and utterly different from us ... yet he is in our midst. This is the main point of the Tabernacle; it emphasises two ideas:

- the idea that God is completely separate from us;
- the idea that God is in our midst.

We would think, as some religions do, that God is so separate from us that he could not possibly speak to us directly or become involved in our affairs; that he would send his Scriptures and his prophets to tell us how to obey him. But the whole Bible is the story of how God involves himself very closely in the affairs of humankind and of his love for us.

God is Separate

> *He who is the blessed and only potentate, the King of kings and Lord of lords, [16] who alone has immortality, dwelling in unapproachable light, whom no man has seen or can see, to whom be honour and everlasting power. Amen.*
>
> *(1 Timothy 6: 15, 16)*

He is the *blessed and only potentate*, the absolute ruler. Psalm 2 and many other places speak of how God will one day establish his rule in power and dominion over the whole earth; he is so powerful that he could squash us like flies if he wanted. Isaiah says that nations are a drop in a bucket to God (Isaiah 40: 15) and Psalm 8: 4 asks: *What is man that You are mindful of him?*

He is *King of kings and Lord of lords*. When Jesus stood before Pilate, the Roman Governor in Jerusalem (John 19: 10, 11), Pilate said, *I have power to crucify You, and power to release You.* Jesus responded, *You could have no power at all against Me unless it had been given you from above.* There is no power on earth, political, economic or military that is not permitted by God. When Jesus appears in glory in Revelation 19, he wears a banner that says *King of kings and Lord of lords.*

He alone has immortality. We see this in the miracles Jesus performed and especially in his own resurrection, but these are only attributes of God. Immortality is more fundamental to him than that. God is the source of life – its very origin. The Creation is described as coming from his Word, that is to say it came out of his imagination. His name is Yahweh, meaning 'I am' – he exists and has life in himself.

He lives in unapproachable light, whom no man has seen or can see. Much of what I discuss in this book is about people encountering God: Moses, Isaiah and others, but in reality, God revealed himself to them. He summoned Isaiah into a vision; he beckoned to Moses out of a burning bush – a metaphor for his presence. The same goes for all the other prophets who met God. We cannot approach God or see him in his natural form. The fact that he created the universe suggests that he exists outside it, so he is literally inaccessible unless he chooses to show himself to us.

The Tabernacle was built to emphasise the separation of God and the things that were dedicated to him from the ordinary world. The presence of Yahweh in the Most Holy Place was carefully protected; only the High Priest was allowed to enter there, once a year and with great care.

The priests and Levites also had to be specially cleansed before they could carry out their religious duties, and when things broke down, the consequences were extreme (see Leviticus 10: 1-3). God revealed himself with fire to purify and to destroy anything that was not holy.

The Tabernacle reinforces the idea that holy things and unholy things are incompatible; in fact, they're like matter and anti-matter: they will destroy each other. Yet Yahweh placed himself right at the centre of the Israelites' camp.

God is Close

When God revealed himself to Moses in Exodus 3, he told him his name:

> *Then Moses said to God, "Indeed, when I come to the children of Israel and say to them, 'The God of your fathers has sent me to you,' and they say to me, 'What is His name?' what shall I say to them?"*
>
> [14] *And God said to Moses, "I AM WHO I AM." And He said, "Thus you shall say to the children of Israel, 'I AM has sent me to you.'"*
>
> *(Exodus 3: 13, 14)*

Whenever we see God in the Bible he is always involved with people. Perhaps this isn't surprising since the Bible is a collection of books written by people about God. God can be known; although he lives in unapproachable light, he shines that light into the world.

At some point after God created the world, darkness was upon the face of the deep, and God said: 'Let there be light' (Genesis 1: 2, 3). This is not a case of simple illumination – the sun comes later (v.14) – but of light and darkness. As John says *God is light and in Him is no darkness at all* (1 John 1: 5).

> *The earth was without form, and void; and darkness was on the face of the deep. And the Spirit of God was hovering over the face of the waters.*
>
> *[3] Then God said, "Let there be light"; and there was light. [4] And God saw the light, that it was good; and God divided the light from the darkness.*
>
> *(Genesis 1: 2-4)*

The light and the darkness in Genesis 1 – and in the rest of the Bible – are spiritual light and darkness; they are opposing entities. When darkness was upon the face of the deep it was a thing that existed, not the absence of something. When the light shone into it, the darkness *did not comprehend i*t (John 1: 5).

This is always true. Darkness brings confusion, chaos, fear and the blurring of boundaries; light brings order and distinction. It brings knowledge and wisdom. God separated the light from the darkness.

Moses was in a state of personal darkness when he was in Midian. Although he had once had a strong sense of purpose, he had been out of circulation for so long that he must have thought his opportunity was lost. Then God spoke to him.

When God reveals himself to Moses as Yahweh, he shows himself as a person and invites Moses into a relationship with him. In fact, I AM is an interesting and perplexing name: a riddle. It invites questions: What are you? Who are you? (Saul's question in Acts 9: 5). And these questions draw us into a relationship with him as we seek answers. We see this in the lives of David and Solomon who spent their lives in a quest to know God better.

Yahweh gives tantalising glimpses of his character. I am: *the LORD who heals you* (Exodus 15: 26); *The LORD who Provides* (Genesis 22: 14); *The Lord, your shepherd* (Psalm 23: 1); *The LORD, your righteousness* (Jeremiah 23: 6); *The LORD of Hosts*, [meaning Yahweh of the armies of heaven] (1 Samuel 1: 3 and many places).

Jesus

> *The Word became flesh, and did tabernacle among us, and we beheld his glory, glory as of an only begotten of a father, full of grace and truth.*
>
> *(John 1: 14 YLT)*

> *For it is the God who commanded light to shine out of darkness, who has shone in our hearts to give the light of the knowledge of the glory of God in the face of Jesus Christ.*
>
> *(2 Corinthians 4: 6)*

In the same way that the Word of God shone light into the darkness of the beginning of the world, he shines light into our darkness too – like Moses – and he reveals Christ to us.

In the passage, we looked at in 1 Timothy 6, the He in verse 15 refers to Jesus. He alone dwells in unapproachable light.

The ultimate way in which God has revealed himself to us, extended his hand to us, is in Jesus Christ. We cannot know God unless he shows himself to us. In the Old Testament, he revealed himself to particular individuals on behalf of the rest of the people, often to commission them with a special assignment (like Moses) or a message (like Isaiah).

But in Jesus Christ God has poured the fulness of himself into a human being (Colossians 2: 9). He lived a 'normal' life on earth, subject to all the same pressures that we are; everything we can know about God is revealed in Jesus.

I used an unusual translation of John 1: 14 above (Young's Literal Translation) because it uses the exact word for what God did in Jesus: he *tabernacled* – literally he pitched his tent in our midst.

The Tabernacle

We can use the ancient Jewish Tabernacle as an illustration of the process of worship because it highlights the holiness of God – that he is separate and also close. We can think of it as a journey into the Presence of God.

At the actual Tabernacle, only priests and Levites could go inside[5], and no one could go in without the blood of a sacrifice being spilled. For us, Jesus' blood cleanses us from sin and fulfils all the ancient sacrifices. Before we can worship, we have to meet Jesus at the cross.

Description
There was a large courtyard in the centre of the Israelite camp, 50 by 25 metres, screened off by a tall linen fence supported by poles. At the eastern end – the front – was a curtain that served as the entrance.

Just inside the curtain was a large bronze altar on which sacrifices were made by the priests; beyond that was a 'laver' – a large vessel containing water – where the priests could wash before doing their religious duties.

The Tabernacle itself was a large tent, 15 by 5 metres and 3 metres high at the eaves. This was made of wooden boards supported by poles and covered with various layers of linen and animal skin. The Tabernacle contained the Sanctuary, where the priests carried out their duties before God each day. It was divided into two parts, the first, the Holy Place, contained the seven-fold lamp, the menorah, a table with bread on it and a small altar for burning incense. Beyond a thick dividing curtain – the veil – was the Most Holy Place where the Ark of the Covenant was. The Ark was a wooden box overlaid with gold with two moulded cherubim on the lid, between which was the presence of God.

A journey into worship

1. We go through the outer curtain and into the *courtyard*. Where at one time the priests would have been sacrificing bulls and goats, we see the Cross of Jesus. Without his sacrifice, we can't approach God. His blood cleanses us from sin and we must remember this as we come to worship.

Unless we accept the sacrifice of Jesus for ourselves, we can go no further. We cannot approach God without our sins cleansed, but as we accept Jesus as our Saviour, we can leave our burdens – our troubles, sicknesses, guilt, fear – at the foot of the cross because these are not holy and have no place in the Sanctuary.

2. Passing *the place of sacrifice*, we meet a group of people standing at the entrance to the Holy Place, singing praises and thanks to God[6]. We join them.

3. With praise and thanksgiving in our hearts, we pass into the *Sanctuary* – into the Holy Place. In the Tabernacle, the walls are hung with richly decorated curtains[7]. To the left is the menorah, to the right, a table with bread on it, and at the far end, a small altar for burning incense. All our senses are engaged: the sound of singing; the smell of the incense; the unsteady light of the

lamps and the designs on the walls; the taste and texture of the bread. These all represent our worship and meditations on God.

For us, guided into worship by the Holy Spirit, we continue to praise as we lose sight of the things of the world that dominate our lives, and concentrate on God. Here we bring our expressions of worship to add to the offerings of those around us: our voices, our service.

In this place, we may hear God speaking to us through spiritual gifts – tongues, prophecy, gifts of knowledge and wisdom – and this will be to build us up as his people, to strengthen, encourage and correct us.

4. Past the *incense altar* – incense represents prayer – and through the curtain that was torn from the top to the bottom when Jesus died, and is no longer a barrier, we enter the *Most Holy Place*.

Perhaps we were expecting a view similar to Isaiah's vision, instead we see Jesus who (we realise) has been beside us the whole time. Now we see him in a new light, not only crucified for our sin but exalted to the highest place, *far above all heavens* (Ephesians 4: 10); *far above all principality and power and might and dominion, and every name that is named* (Ephesians 1: 21) because *he dwells in unapproachable light*.

He is the one we love, yet – just like Isaiah – we fall before him until he touches our shoulder and says: 'It's me – don't be afraid' and speaks to us.

In the ancient Tabernacle, the Ark of the Covenant was in the place of a throne, the place where God 'sat', except it wasn't really like a chair. The space on the top, between the golden cherubim was where the presence of God was, above the box containing the stone tablets on which the Ten Commandments were written.

The Ark, isolated behind its veil in the Most Holy Place of the Tabernacle, shows the separation of Yahweh from the people, his holiness through four distinct stages of separation. The screen from the Israelite camp into the outer court; the Altar where the priests would make sacrifices; the door of the Holy Place, the Sanctuary, where the lights shone in the darkness and the incense was offered. Finally, once a year with great caution, the High Priest would enter the Most Holy Place to meet the presence of Yahweh face to face.

But for all this elaborate separation, and the ritual and Law that surrounded it, the Ark, the presence of God between the cherubim, was right in the middle of the camp only a few metres away from where ordinary people lived their lives. When they moved, they moved together.

What does God say to us?

Previously we've looked at Psalm 95 (*Today ... do not harden your heart*) and Isaiah 6 (*Whom shall I send? Go*). God speaks to us personally, inviting us to accompany him in friendship and partnership as he extends his love to the world. Through our worship, he requires a response, firstly to examine ourselves and then to be open to what he says.

In the Sanctuary God speaks no word of judgement or condemnation to us. The judgement that would have fallen on us fell instead on Jesus. If we accept him as our saviour, we are free from guilt. We come to seek his face and worship him. He speaks to us and sends us out once more to be his ambassadors (2 Corinthians 5: 20).

Discussion 4

How do you understand 'holiness'?

- How is God close to us today?
- How is he separate from us?

In Ephesians 4, Paul talks about 'the unity of the Spirit and the bond of peace' (vv. 1-6).

- How is the church you serve united?
- Are there ways in which it is disunited?
- How can you demonstrate the unity of the Spirit and the bond of peace?

What is your experience of leading others in worship?

How well to you measure up to Paul's leadership criteria in 1 Timothy 3: 1-13?

- Do you basically think of yourself as a 'saint' or a 'sinner'?
- How can we lead 'invisibly'

5. The Outer Court

> *I will praise You, O LORD, among the peoples,*
> *And I will sing praises to You among the nations.*
> *For Your mercy is great above the heavens,*
> *And Your truth reaches to the clouds.*
>
> *(Psalm 108: 3, 4)*

In the last chapter, we looked at worship using a model of the ancient Jewish Tabernacle. In this and the next two chapters, we're going to take a closer look at what that means for us as worshippers.

Worship in the outer court is our first encounter with God, when he meets with us and we turn to him. For us there is no altar for sacrifices as there was in the ancient Tabernacle; we come to the cross of Jesus Christ, the ultimate sacrifice, who cleanses us from sin and gives us access to God, our heavenly Father. In this chapter, we'll attempt to answer the following questions:

- What is worship in the outer court like?
- Who worships in the outer court?
- Where does it fit into our worship?
- How does it lead us to a deeper understanding of God?

We've previously looked at Psalm 95 in three sections; these match the three areas of the Tabernacle. Verses 1-5 are an invitation to worship – *Come, let us sing unto the LORD* (v.1) – and a celebration of the majesty of God; they describe worship in the outer court. Verses 6 and 7a are an invitation to draw nearer to God in his

Holy Place – *Oh come, let us worship and bow down* (v.6) – and the rest of the Psalm is what God says to us when we're in his presence and how we respond to it. We can call this the Most Holy Place, although Jesus has removed the division and through his blood, we always have direct access to God.

> *Let us draw near with a true heart in full assurance of faith, having our hearts sprinkled from an evil conscience and our bodies washed with pure water.*
>
> (Hebrews 10: 22)

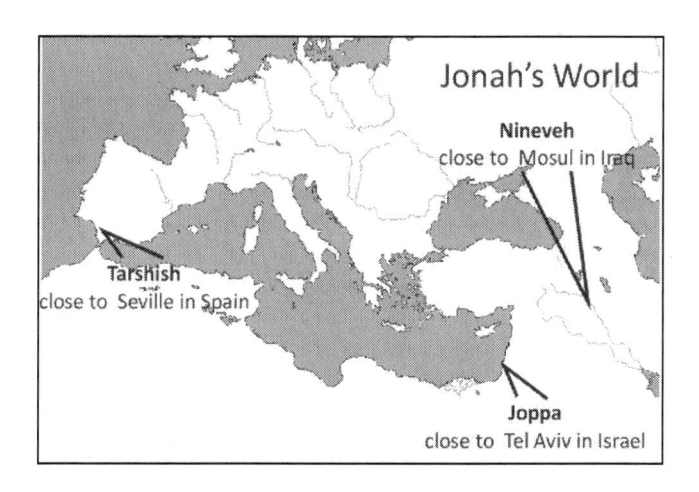

Jonah's World

Nineveh
close to Mosul in Iraq

Tarshish
close to Seville in Spain

Joppa
close to Tel Aviv in Israel

Jonah 1: Approaching Worship

This will seem to be a digression – but please bear with me.

In the Book of Jonah chapter 1, God speaks to Jonah and shares something that is troubling him. The issue is the wickedness of Nineveh, which is an offence to him. Jonah's task is to go and 'cry out' against it.

Nineveh was the capital city of the Assyrian empire which was feared and dreaded by the people of Israel with good reason: they destroyed cities, plundered wealth, committed acts of genocide and trafficked slaves. Jonah probably thought that if God was angry with them, that was a good thing. He had no intention of warning them and tried to get as far away as possible. In a straight line, Nineveh was about seven hundred miles north-east of Joppa; Tarshish was nearly two thousand miles to the west.

So, Jonah finds himself on a ship with a big storm brewing up (v.4) and a lot of foreign sailors who don't know Yahweh. They're all frightened and the desperate sailors shout to their various gods for help (v.5 NLT). When the captain finds Jonah in the bottom of the boat, he orders him to *Get up and pray to your God! Maybe he will pay attention to us and spare our lives* (v.6 NLT).

At this point Jonah is feeling very far from holy. He's cold, wet, scared and trying to find a hole to crawl into because he knows that God is onto him. And, being a Jew, he most certainly doesn't want to pray in the company of a lot of idol-worshipping Gentiles. He may even be thinking that drowning is better than going to Nineveh.

The sailors, possibly as part of their own prayers, cast lots to see who they can blame for the storm: it falls on Jonah (v.7); they demand an explanation.

> *I am a Hebrew; and I fear the LORD, the God of heaven, who made the sea and the dry land.*
>
> *(Jonah 1: 9)*

When asked directly, Jonah speaks and gives the essence of a testimony. His words change the meaning of the storm and of the sailors' fears because it puts them into the context of the God of heaven, who made the sea; he also tells them (v.10) that he's running away from Yahweh.

And he tells them quite plainly that they'll have to get rid of him in order to survive (v.12) but the sailors are even more worried by that suggestion: it might make matters worse! Their determination to row for safety has more to do with their fear of blood-guilt than any great regard for Jonah (13, 14). They were pagans (probably Greeks, Phoenicians or Egyptians) who honoured their various deities of Earth, Sea and Sky. In some respects, they seem more devout than Jonah or at least, more terrified of their gods. They would not have had a clearly developed theology but would have had an acute sense of 'what goes around comes around'. They didn't want to be responsible for Jonah's death because the possible consequences would have been terrible.

Jonah has to persuade them that it's Yahweh who controls the sea, not Poseidon. The proof of this will be when they throw him overboard. The sailors have to take a huge leap of faith: do they trust the gods that they have been brought up to believe in and honour every day, or do they trust the God of an awkward stranger?

In the end, they throw him overboard with a prayer to Yahweh: *We pray, O LORD, please do not let us perish for this man's life, and do not charge us with innocent blood; for You, O LORD, have done as it pleased You* (v.14). The sailors turn to God.

> *Then the men feared the LORD exceedingly, and offered a sacrifice to the LORD and took vows.*
>
> *(Jonah 1: 16)*

In the first chapter of Jonah a disobedient servant of God got onto a ship to run as far away as possible from what God was telling him to do. In order to stop him, God sent a storm that threatened the lives of the men who were with him. They were afraid and sought the truth at first by calling on their own gods, then finally calling on Yahweh when Jonah had explained who he was.

They had to respond to God in faith – and they risked everything to do it.

The outcome was that Jonah went to a place where God had his full attention and the sailors turned to God with vows and sacrifices. This is what I am calling 'Worship in the Outer Court'.

What is worship 'in the outer court' like?

1. *Worship in the outer court is accessible by everyone.* All the people in this story know their need for God in a general way; they can tell that something spiritual is happening, but not exactly what. Jonah, in spite of his disobedience and generally sorry state gives the people a clear route into God's presence by stating the truth very simply about who he is and who God is. As testimonies go, Jonah's sounds very 'thin', especially since he's running away from God! But Jonah's word is exactly what's needed. He goes on to explain exactly what they have to do to be saved. They do this; the storm ends, and they know that God did it.

This is *evangelism*: declaring the good news of salvation to people who are lost. Isaiah said: *the LORD hath anointed me to preach good tidings unto the meek* (Isaiah 61: 1 KJV). The meek are those who know they need it. The outer court of the ancient Tabernacle was dominated by the altar; for us, this is Jesus' Cross. Worship in the outer court meets people where they are and takes them to where Jesus is.

At the very least, worship in the outer court gives everyone there a snapshot of their lives in relation to the Almighty God.

Worship in the outer court is accessible to everyone because Jesus is accessible to everyone. It might seem a bit surprising that I'm calling the interaction between Jonah, the sailors and God 'worship'. It doesn't look like a 'meeting' – and if you asked them, they wouldn't even have agreed about which 'god' they were worshipping, at least to start with. Through the reluctant testimony of Jonah, God met them and saved their lives and their souls as they worshipped him.

2. *Worship in the outer court states truths about God and humankind.* In this story, the attributes of God are displayed for people to see.

His mercy. When the sailors do what Jonah says and throw him overboard, calm is restored immediately. But the bigger picture is important too: why was Jonah running away? God wanted him to be a messenger of peace and salvation to Nineveh. He didn't want to do it, but God's mercy was bigger than Jonah's fear and hatred.

His power and his personality. Yahweh isn't a god that Jonah has made up, nor was he some ancestral cult – he speaks personally and reasonably to Jonah, explaining his motives (Jonah 1: 2; Jonah 4: 10, 11) and expects Jonah to be reasonable with him in return. When that doesn't work, he uses the power of nature and the actions of other people to teach Jonah a valuable lesson about compassion.

3. *Worship in the outer court leads us to Jesus' Cross.* The outcome of the sailors' experience of Jonah was that they encountered the true God. He revealed himself to them in ways that they could understand and gave them the opportunity to respond; then they offered a sacrifice to him and 'took vows' (Jonah 1: 16).

We know that God wants all people to live in fellowship with him, and to know him personally, but before this can happen, we must first come to Jesus and understand that he is able to save us: we cannot by-pass the cross. The cross is the foundation of our worship; we can't move into a closer relationship with God without going through it, claiming Jesus' blood as cleansing for our own sins.

Who worships in the Outer Court?

> *Those who come to God must believe that he exists and that he rewards those who seek him diligently*
>
> *(Hebrews 11: 6)*

The simple answer to that question is *everyone*.

1. *Christians in need of refreshment.* This might be people like Jonah, who are actively trying to stay out of God's way. God used Jonah in spite of himself, and in leading the sailors to God (which he did accidentally), he moved into a place where God could bring him to his senses.

Sometimes we can become weary and perhaps hard of heart as we serve God. We can become tired of service, even battle-weary with spiritual warfare. Sometimes in our desire to serve we can lose our focus and dependence on the Holy Spirit. We need to come into his Holy Place, his Sanctuary, into a closer place of worship where we can be refreshed.

Psalms 42 and 43 describe this experience of 'dryness' – when even worship among God's people seems flat and dull. In Psalm 43 the writer says:

Oh, send out Your light and Your truth!
Let them lead me;
Let them bring me to Your holy hill
And to Your tabernacle.

⁴ Then I will go to the altar of God,
To God my exceeding joy;
And on the harp I will praise You,
O God, my God.

(Psalm 43: 3, 4)

Refreshing ourselves at the cross and on the reality of God's promises begins to renew our joy: *I shall yet praise him, who is the health of my countenance, and my God* (Psalm 42: 11 KJV).

2. *People seeking God*. The captain of the ship, perhaps because he is responsible for the safety of the crew and the cargo, is very eager that everyone – particularly Jonah – calls on God for help (*Arise, call on your God,* v.6). The sailors, too, are very keen to find out what is happening after Jonah pulled the short straw (*Please tell us: who's responsible; who are you and where are you from?* v.8).

Because worship in the outer court is based on evangelism – on directing people to Jesus' cross – it is available to everyone. Whether they progress into the Holy Place or not depends on how they respond to the cross. The sailors ended their episode in Jonah 1 with a sacrifice and vows to Yahweh. They didn't have a priest or the correct rituals, nor did they have the Temple or the

Tabernacle, they simply worshipped because they believed the truth.

3. *Everyone else.* In order to approach God, we must believe that he exists. That sounds obvious, but if we don't believe in him, we're probably not going to find him. The pagan sailors believed: their faith was misdirected and needed to be focused on the God who made the sea, but undoubtedly, they had a measure of faith.

We must also believe that it's worth calling out to him. The sailors were desperate for salvation, but sometimes people can be cynical or bitter because of the hurt they've suffered. We sometimes have to show such people the love and compassion of Christ before they can reach out to God. Many people are afraid – and often fear comes from ignorance and the unknown. When we feel out of control, we are afraid. God's love conquers fear:

> *There is no fear in love, but perfect love cast out fear.*
>
> *(1 John 4: 18)*

Where does this fit into our worship?

The first chapter of Jonah is not a worship service but a hastily arranged 'crying-out-to-God-in-desperation' session. God doesn't like it when we are desperate; he doesn't enjoy our pain and fear, but sometimes it's only when we're really hurting that we are open to him. He wants us to know his peace and to have confidence in the truth of his Word.

God deals with us in truth.

Jonah shows us that God will find us and speak to us anywhere. It's often through these times of pain and distress that God strips away the layers of our defences and takes us to the bedrock of truth. When we're at the bottom we find God – in the belly of a fish for example.

When we come to lead worship, at each point we must be open to what God will do; also, whether we are planning a service or just playing a small part, we must make Jesus' cross the focus. Like the altar in the Tabernacle and the point at which the sailors had to throw Jonah off the ship, the cross of Jesus is our *point of truth*. We can look at it from a distance and go no further, or we can help people to hear what God through his Holy Spirit is saying and enter his presence.

Some church services never go beyond the outer court because they never invite the people to meet Jesus; the cross remains at a distance. Some Christians have never gone beyond this point because, while they have looked at Jesus, they have never met with him personally or understood fully who he is.

Worship in the outer court, is the first stage in our meeting with God.

How does it lead us into a deeper understanding of Christ?

> *Therefore they cried out to the* LORD *and said,*
> *"We pray, O* LORD, *please do not let us perish*

> *for this man's life, and do not charge us with
> innocent blood; for You, O LORD, have done as it
> pleased You.*

(Jonah 1: 14)

Fear turns into trust. In the height of the storm the sailors were terrified that they were going to drown and also that they had incurred the anger of the gods in some way. Through Jonah's testimony, this basic fear of the unknown was turned into the fear of Yahweh, *they cried out to the LORD* (Jonah 1: 14). On the face of it this might not look like an improvement, but the basic difference is that Yahweh is *the God of heaven, who made the sea*. Whatever relationship the sailors had to their various gods, Jonah knows Yahweh: he doesn't seem to like him very much, but the reality of this relationship gives the sailors hope. The fear of death and the fear of the Lord are not the same thing because the fear of the Lord has hope (see also 1 Chronicles 21: 13 – *Let me fall into the hand of the LORD, for His mercies are very great*).

This thin glimmer of light is enough; by the end of the incident, when the storm has subsided, they put their trust in him when they make vows.

> *I sought the LORD and he heard me, and
> delivered me from all my fears.*

(Psalm 34: 4)

When we trust God in a crisis and come out the other side, our relationship with him changes. Jesus' disciples had a similar experience in a boat:

> *And a great windstorm arose, and the waves beat into the boat, so that it was already filling.* ³⁸ *But He was in the stern, asleep on a pillow. And they awoke Him and said to Him, "Teacher, do You not care that we are perishing?"*
>
> ³⁹ *Then He arose and rebuked the wind, and said to the sea, "Peace, be still!" And the wind ceased and there was a great calm.* ⁴⁰ *But He said to them, "Why are you so fearful? How is it that you have no faith?"* ⁴¹ *And they feared exceedingly, and said to one another, "Who can this be, that even the wind and the sea obey Him!"*
>
> *(Mark 4: 37-41)*

The disciples, just like Jonah's sailors, move from fear of death to awe at the power that Jesus demonstrates when he calms the storm with a word.

Fear belongs to darkness. We fear when we have no control; when we lack understanding or when we are faced with the unknown. The fear of death dominates most of human experience most of the time (Hebrews 2: 15). God speaks light into the darkness of the storm and creates order:

> *God who commanded light to shine out of darkness, ... has shone in our hearts to give the light of the knowledge of the glory of God in the face of Jesus Christ.*
>
> *(2 Corinthians 4: 6)*

As we give control to him in the midst of madness and despair, he gives control back to us when the sea is calm again.

When the storm ceased, the sailors – like the disciples – had no doubt that God was at work. In each case they were able to worship him in a new and deeper way.

Jonah also moved on to worship God in new ways. When he hit the water, he thought he was dead – and being swallowed by a fish probably didn't change his opinion, but later, *Jonah cried out to God from inside the fish* (Jonah 2: 1).

His situation is different from the sailors', or even the disciples'; he knew that Yahweh had called him to go to Nineveh but had other plans. God had a lesson to teach him about his love and compassion to the non-Jews, even those who were feared enemies – and this is another fear that the love and light of God dispels.

God wants us to change by having our minds renewed (Romans 12: 2). He's willing to deal with us like disobedient children by having us tipped out of the boat, but he'd rather speak with us like adults. When God speaks to Jonah, he tries to involve him in his concern for the people of Nineveh (Jonah 4: 11), not only to stop them sinning; he wants their salvation and he wants Jonah to want it too. To Jonah, the devout Jew, the idea of pitying Nineveh was impossible to grasp.

Inside the fish Jonah has some 'face-time' with God. It's his Holy Place where Yahweh has taken him aside to speak to him personally; he has to refocus his heart, and he starts off by acknowledging that wherever he has gone, God has found him:

> *I cried out to the LORD because of my affliction, and He answered me. Out of the belly of Sheol I cried, and You heard my voice.*

(Jonah 2: 2)

All of Jonah's prayer inside the fish is taken from other Scriptures. It's as if he's fallen down to the lowest point he could go and has landed on his foundation, which is the Word of God, built up inside him over years of study and meditation. Some find it surprising that he doesn't repent from his disobedience at this point – but he's not ready to do that and even by the end of chapter 4, although he's stopped running away, he's still angry. His problem is that he can't believe that God will be gracious to Gentiles.

He finishes up by restating a promise he has previously made to God; like the sailors:

> *I will offer sacrifices to you with songs of praise, and I will fulfil all my vows. For my salvation comes from the LORD alone.*

(Jonah 2: 9)

Worshiping in the outer court has brought the captain and the sailors, and Jonah in a different way, into a place where God is able to speak to them and where they are able to respond.

Worship in the Outer Court

Worship in the outer court is our first point of contact with God. It can be in a worship service or anywhere that circumstances bring us to encounter him. God always meets with us on the basis of truth and reality – this is why he often meets with us at our point of greatest need or fear.

When we plan a service, we cannot predict how God will meet people, but we can, by being prayerful and thoughtful, make an environment where a meeting is likely to take place.

Worship in the outer court should be based on praise and celebration of who God is (reflecting Psalm 95: 1-5).

It should also be centred on the cross of Jesus Christ. It should direct worshippers to Jesus and call them to salvation first and also to refocus their lives on him. Worship in the outer court must invite everyone to move through the cross, embracing cleansing in Jesus' blood, into a close personal relationship with him.

We've also seen that personal testimony is powerful. Jonah wasn't exactly glowing with love for God, yet his simple statement of who he was in relation to Yahweh: *I am a Hebrew; and I fear the LORD, the God of heaven, who made the sea and the dry land* had the effect of opening a door for the sailors to be saved. Our expectation should be that people will come to Christ and be saved.

Discussion 5

What does 'worship in the outer court' look like in your setting?

Within the 'outer court' there is movement towards Jesus' cross.

Suggest some songs or some words that might be right to use in 'the outer court'.

Obviously, if we know we're going to 'lead worship', we have to plan it diligently. To what extent can we expect God to 'do his own thing' regardless of our preparation?

Write down some words or phrases that speak to you of God's greatness. Can you form these into verse – perhaps a lyric?

6. The Sanctuary (the Holy Place) part 1

> *"Come now, and let us reason together," says the LORD, "though your sins are like scarlet, they shall be as white as snow; though they are red like crimson, they shall be as wool."*
>
> *(Isaiah 1: 18)*

God has revealed himself as a person, someone that we can know. In the last chapter, we saw how Jonah's relationship with Yahweh, even though he was running away from him, was a ray of light to the sailors in a very dark and difficult place. It led to them being saved physically and spiritually.

As we worship in the outer court, God invites us to meet him and to know him. If we've never met him before, we can come to Jesus' cross and be 'saved' as we experience his love for the first time; if we know him already it's an opportunity for us to refresh and refocus ourselves on the basics of the gospel.

God sent his Son, Jesus, as a perfect sacrifice to remove our sin and guilt completely so there is nothing to stop us knowing God for ourselves. That's the gospel – the Good News. If we accept Jesus' death as a sacrifice for our sins – his innocent blood in our place – we have fellowship with God. *We are adopted into his own family* (Ephesians 1: 5 NLT).

Moving into the Sanctuary

Thinking of the ancient Tabernacle once again, we move past the place of sacrifice – for them the Altar; for us the Cross – and into the Tabernacle itself. The larger of its two rooms is the *Sanctuary* or *Holy Place*.

Everything in this place has been dedicated to God: all the materials used to construct it; the gold and the acacia wood used to make the furniture; the oil that is burned in the lamp, the flour to make the bread and the special incense burned on the altar. Even the people – the priests and Levites who work here have a special preparation – special clothes and anointings that single them out for service before they enter.

There is no natural light in the Sanctuary; all the light comes from the *seven-fold lampstand*, the *menorah*, which stands to the left as we enter, and is never extinguished. This represents the light of God that shines into the darkness; for us the light is the Holy Spirit, who first appeared among the disciples as *tongues of fire* in Acts 2: 3. The Holy Spirit is the Spirit of Jesus, the light of the world (John 8: 12); the constant witness of God among the people; his light shining into us.

A version of the lampstand appears in Revelation 1: 12-20 where John turns and sees *seven golden lampstands* and Jesus Christ moving between them. The lampstands, he says, represent seven churches that John will write letters to – and also the whole of the Church of God throughout time and space with Christ at its centre.

To the right, as we enter, is *the table of 'show-bread'*. This is a small table made of wood and overlaid with gold on which the priests place twelve loaves of bread – one to represent each Tribe of Israel. These are loaves of flat unleavened bread like matzos or wafers; each Sabbath priests or Levites bake fresh loaves and place them on the table where they stay for a week before being eaten in the Sanctuary and new loaves brought to replace them.

The bread illustrates two things. Firstly, the provision of God: Jesus taught us to pray, *give us today our daily bread* (Matthew 6: 11). In each loaf God is promising to provide for an entire Tribe of the people.

Secondly, it illustrates God's willingness to share in our every-day needs. As the priests share the bread weekly in the presence of God, it shows his presence at the heart of the community to meet with the people and provide for their needs. In the Gospels, Jesus shared meals with all sorts of people – rich, poor, righteous and unrighteous, sometimes producing food miraculously when none was available. Afterwards he left us, the church, with the 'breaking of bread', the Communion, through which we are reminded of his death (1 Corinthians 11: 23-34).

Jesus says *I am the bread of life* (John 6: 48). Bread is a powerful symbol of God meeting our physical and Spiritual needs.

Finally, at the far end of the Sanctuary, in front of the veil that separates the Most Holy Place, is another small altar – *the incense altar*. Here, specially prepared incense is burned before the presence of God. This represents the constant prayers and worship of the people before him.

The fragrance of the incense is almost overpowering; it soaks into the fabric of the tent and the clothes of anyone inside.

This rich fragrance (or something similar) is mentioned in John 12 where Mary breaks a jar of expensive perfume over Jesus' feet and the smell fills the house. Most of us don't use incense today as part of worship because it represents something that is actually present – the Holy Spirit making intercession for his people (Romans 8: 27).

People who come into our church building often comment on how 'peaceful' or 'nice' it feels, even when there's no meeting (and even when the heating isn't on). There's nothing special about the building; we do good coffee but otherwise it's just a big room. We don't burn candles or incense and there's not much polished wood or anything else to smell 'religious'; but it's a place where God has been worshipped simply for many years. Our church isn't alone in this – it's a common thing where Christ is worshipped. It's a lingering sense of the presence of God.

When we worship God, his presence is *tangible* – we can feel it. This is not surprising, because he's real. Some people think of the Holy Spirit as an attitude to life – the holy attitude. It can be helpful to think of him in this way, but he is more than that. The Holy Spirit who lives in us is a Person; he moved on the face of the water in Creation and breathed life into Adam; he is the breath of God; his very Presence. Just like us, when we leave a whiff of ourselves in a very bodily way, he changes the atmosphere in a room – and people can sense it.

(I'm not talking about people who get tingly feelings or see mists and lights. People 'see' all sorts of things in different places, and sometimes they hallucinate. There's nothing 'woo' about the Holy Spirit.)

The incense, like the lamps and the bread, represents the presence of God among his people. Everything in the Sanctuary speaks of God engaging closely with his people: his light, his provision, our worship and his Presence.

Blockages to worship

Unfortunately, a lot of people leave worship in the outer court; they go no further than the cross. They never enter the sanctuary where God wants to meet with them in person. Sometimes when we lead, we do everything right, but it just doesn't 'happen'; sometimes leading worship can be very hard work – like wading through thick mud. Why is worship sometimes blocked?

There could be several reasons for this.

- I'd love to worship, but I'm so stressed at the moment, I've no space left in my head.

Others might say:

- I'm saved now: I'm safe. I'm going to heaven, what more do I need?
- I'm so grateful that Jesus died in my place, but I really can't expect any more from God.

- I believe that Jesus forgave me, but I keep sinning. I have bad thoughts. I'm not very holy; I don't think I can go any deeper with God. I have to keep coming back here to the cross.

Let's think about these doubts that everyone has from time to time. They can hinder us from moving on with God.

I'd love to worship ...

... but I'm so stressed at the moment, I've no space left in my head.

Sometimes people struggle to worship because they are preoccupied with troublesome thoughts, or are stressed, anxious or depressed. This is a big subject that needs much fuller development than I can give it here.

For people suffering from stress, anxiety or depression, worship, prayer and Bible study can be very difficult. These are common problems, but it's necessary to say that – unless the Holy Spirit gives insight – those who have not suffered in this way will find it hard to empathise with those who have.

If you're feeling under pressure, you may find it hard to concentrate; you might feel low. You may not be able to 'snap out of it' and you might have made yourself patterns of thinking and behaviour where you feel safe, but which are isolating. You may find it hard to speak about it; this may not be a good thing (and you certainly do need to speak to your doctor and your pastor). It might seem unlikely, but worshipping with God's people is a good thing to do. His presence heals. Even if you find it impossible to take part and just sit at the back, taking your eyes away from your troubles and resting them on God and his promises for a while is refreshing; in the words of Psalm 23, it restores my soul. It will help you to see your situation in the light of God's love and provision.

Psalms 42 and 43 understand this:

> *Why are you cast down, O my soul?*
> *And why are you disquieted within me*
> *Hope in God, for I shall yet praise Him*
> *For the help of His countenance.*

(Psalm 42: 5)

The writer here is struggling to experience the presence of God and feels dry, longing for refreshment; My soul thirsts for God, for the living God (v.2). He is unmoved by attendance at worship, yet he knows that, in the end, his restoration will come from God.

> *Oh, send out Your light and Your truth!*
> *Let them lead me;*
> *Let them bring me to Your holy hill*
> *And to Your tabernacle.*
>
> *4 Then I will go to the altar of God,*
> *To God my exceeding joy;*
> *And on the harp I will praise You,*
> *O God, my God.*
>
> *5 Why are you cast down, O my soul?*
> *And why are you disquieted within me?*

> *Hope in God; For I shall yet praise Him,*
> *The help of my countenance and my God.*

(Psalm 43: 3-5)

It will be the light and truth of God that returns the psalmist to health and restores his ability to worship; but where he is at the moment, God must make the first move because he is unable to.

The theme that runs through these Psalms is *Hope in God, for I shall yet praise Him*. I can't do it right now, even though I want to, but I will do sometime soon.

If you're feeling low, putting yourself in among God's people is important, even if you can't participate right now. It is God who heals and who restores, and the gifts that he has placed in his church (see ahead, Chapter 13) will work to build you up.

I'm saved now...

... I'm safe. I'm going to heaven.

That's a wonderful place to be, because at the bottom of everything in your life now, you have a sense that God has welcomed you; that he's holding you; that *the eternal God is your refuge, and underneath are the everlasting arms* (Deuteronomy 33: 27). This is the most wonderful sense of safety.

But it's like being born again – a phrase that Jesus used in John 3. Spiritually, you're like a baby and you need to grow and become mature. It takes time – a lifetime, in fact – and there is more to know and understand about God than you can imagine. There will always be more to explore of God. This is the reason you were put on earth. Enter in to worship and tell him your heart; allow him to speak to you.

I'm so grateful that Jesus died in my place ...

... but I really can't expect any more from God.

This might be 'English reserve' or shyness. At the very best our lives on earth are mortal, limited by time and three dimensions. They are only a shadow of what exists in God's presence (Hebrews 8: 5). In this physical universe, we can understand only a tiny fraction of what God has made.

Yet God has promised us big things, more than this.

> *[He] has blessed us with every spiritual blessing in the heavenly places in Christ, just as He chose us in Him before the foundation of the world, that we should be holy and without blame before Him in love.*
>
> *(Ephesians 1: 3, 4)*

Ask yourself in these verses: *How many* spiritual blessings has God given me? *When* did God choose me? *Why* did he choose me?

Take a few minutes to read the whole of Ephesians 1 and ask: What is God's promise to me?

Every spiritual blessing. God made you and knows how you tick; he knows exactly what your needs are and how to meet them. He can fill you to the best of your potential because only he really knows what that is. Before the beginning of time, he designed you. He saw your potential for love and creativity so that one day –

today, in fact – you can come before him *holy and blameless in love*.

Is that a bit too much? We are talking about God – and he called you by name.

It's true that the Bible says that we should not take God for granted (Psalm 19: 13) – but he has made himself our most faithful friend. By placing his own life within us (Ephesians 1: 13, 14) he plans to make us holy too (v.18).

I believe that Jesus forgave me …

… but I keep sinning. I have bad thoughts. I'm not very holy; I don't think I can go any deeper with God. I have to keep coming back here to the cross to be forgiven.

All of these are caused by a basic misunderstanding of what Jesus did on the cross. The solution is to keep coming back, not to what your feelings say but to what the Bible says. Feelings of sinfulness will not go away as long as we're human and living in this world and as long as the Holy Spirit keeps doing his work, but the fact of forgiveness is deeper than this. Let's remind ourselves of some basics that might help.

Gospel basics – a reminder

> *All have sinned and fall short of the glory of God.*
>
> *(Romans 3: 23)*

In other words, everybody starts off in the same place. It's helpful not to think of 'sins' as a long list of things we do wrong; the key point is that we fall short of the glory of God. He is holy, eternal, all-powerful and all-knowing: of course, we fall short of his glory. Our sin – our messed-up-ness – prevents us from being holy and acceptable to God. Although he loves us, we can't overcome sin and we're lost without his intervention.

And it's not only stuff that we can't help – our background, environment etc. – at one time or another; we've all deliberately turned our backs on God. We are guilty, as the old Prayer Book says, *through our own deliberate fault*. So, we are damaged by other people's faults, hindered and frustrated by our own faults and morally evil as well, causing offence to God and hurt to others. And instead of seeking God's help straight away, we tried to justify ourselves (It was the woman… It was the Serpent… It's not my fault). *They are altogether become filthy; there is none that doeth good, no, not one* (Psalm 53: 3 KJV). We should die. This is why Jesus came.

> *For when we were still without strength, in due time Christ died for the ungodly. ⁷ For scarcely for a righteous man will one die … ⁸ But God demonstrates His own love toward us, in that while we were still sinners, Christ died for us.*
>
> *(Romans 5: 6-8)*

Christ died for the *ungodly*, not for good people. Jesus said that he came to call sinners, not righteous people. God comes to us where we are; he reaches down into our mess and gives us his hand. We don't have to be good for this to happen; in fact, we have to know we're bad and want to change.

The 'wanting to change' part is important: this is repentance. We turn from our sin, the rubbish that's in us, that falls short of the glory of God. We give it to Jesus. When he died, he paid for it.

> *For He made Him who knew no sin [Jesus] to be sin for us, that we might become the righteousness of God in Him.*
>
> *(2 Corinthians 5: 21)*

Jesus died instead of you and me. He was punished and took the full power of God's anger against sin (watch the film The Passion of the Christ if you're not quite sure what this means) in my place and yours. Jesus knew no sin. It isn't just that he never sinned; it wasn't in him to sin. Although he was tempted in exactly the same ways that we are (think about that) he did not give in to it. Nevertheless, he chose to go to the cross on your behalf and mine.

> *For God so loved the world that He gave His only begotten Son, that whoever believes in Him should not perish [die spiritually] but have everlasting life. [17] For God did not send His Son into the world to condemn the world, but that the world through Him might be saved.*
>
> *(John 3: 16, 17)*

He did this because he loves us, not because of some sort of obligation. Understand this: God loves the world. That is, he loves everyone in the world individually. He does not want us to *perish*; he has gone to extreme lengths so that we won't die and be eternally separated from him, and Jesus' blood proves it.

So, back to feelings of sinfulness and guilt. It may be that the Holy Spirit is prompting you to give more of yourself to him. In this case he will be specific and say exactly what it is that you need to repent of. But if it's a general feeling of 'unworthiness', this is not from God. It's most likely your own doubting mind or it might be the Devil making accusations.

In all three cases, the answer is the same. Whether it's the Holy Spirit, your own mind or the Devil, you need to go back to what the Bible says about sin and forgiveness. Regardless of what you feel, the Bible is God's word on the matter.

> *... if we walk in the light as He is in the light, we have fellowship with one another, and the blood of Jesus Christ His Son cleanses us from all sin.*
>
> *[8] If we say that we have no sin, we deceive ourselves, and the truth is not in us. [9] If we confess our sins, He is faithful and just to forgive us our sins and to cleanse us from all unrighteousness. [10] If we say that we have not sinned, we make Him a liar, and His word is not in us.*

(1 John 1: 7-10)

First: we have to admit that we *have sinned*. To deny that is just wrong – *the truth would not be in us*. Second, we have to confess our sins and trust God that he is faithful and will forgive us. Third, verse 7 says that Jesus' blood *cleanses us from all sin*; v.9 says *all unrighteousness.* 'All' is a big word. There is no sin for which God has not forgiven us.

I say, 'has forgiven' (in the past), because Jesus died 2000 years ago; we don't have to crucify him again. Note that this is easy and simple. It is really easy and simple. There is not some hidden religious code here. God has forgiven us; all we have to do is to accept Jesus. But because it's simple doesn't mean it's cheap. God loves us and bought us back to himself; it cost him everything. And there's the rub.

> *There was no other good enough to pay the price of sin;*
> *He only could unlock the gate of heaven, and let us in.*

(Cecil F. Alexander, 1818-1895)

As we walk in the light as he is in the light, we have fellowship with God and with each other (1 John 1: 7). Walking in the light is a journey and we'll explore elsewhere what the end-point of the journey is, but it doesn't happen all at once. I remember asking a very elderly Christian brother, who had served God as an evangelist and Bible teacher in Africa for many years, if it got any easier. No.

Sometimes we are amazed and disgusted at what comes out of us; sometimes it feels as if we're right back at square-one, but this is why we need to come into worship through the outer court with its focus on the cross. We often have to go right back there. *If we confess our sins ...*

For more on the points discussed above I recommend two of Andrew Wommack's books: *Grace: the power of the gospel* (Wommack, 2007) and *The War Is Over* (Wommack, 2008).

'Drawing near'

We enter worship through the blood of Jesus – nothing else will do. All our cares and the business of the world must be left outside: we are coming to meet with God on his terms. We don't need a special building or a 'tent of meeting'; he meets with us exactly where we are: in our hearts. In fact, the King James Bible sometimes refers to our bodies as tabernacles (2 Corinthians 5: 1-8). We are 'tents of meeting'.

> *How amiable are thy tabernacles, O Lord of Hosts!*[8]
>
> *(Psalm 84: 1 KJV)*

Which could mean: *What a great group of people!*

In the outer court, we've been singing praise and bringing our own issues to him, like the sailors on Jonah's boat. Now we've left those behind at Jesus' Cross, knowing that he is faithful to forgive our sin and to take care of all the burdens of our hearts. Now we enter the presence of God himself.

> *Therefore, brethren, having boldness to enter the Holiest by the blood of Jesus ...* [22] *let us draw*

> *near with a true heart in full assurance of faith, having our hearts sprinkled from an evil conscience and our bodies washed with pure water.* [23] *Let us hold fast the confession of our hope without wavering, for He who promised is faithful* [24] *And let us consider one another in order to stir up love and good works,* [25] *not forsaking the assembling of ourselves together ... but exhorting one another, and so much the more as you see the Day approaching.*
>
> *(Hebrews 10: 22-25)*

There are four things to draw attention to in this:

1. *Having boldness to enter ...in full assurance of faith.* Jesus has secured the way for us – and we must not hold back. We must not go by what we feel but by what the Bible teaches us ... we must enter God's presence by faith.

> *Not having my own righteousness ... but that which is through faith in Christ, the righteousness which is from God by faith.*
>
> *(Philippians 3: 9)*

Jesus, just as he did on earth, is inviting us to a feast. The point of worship in the sanctuary is not that our needs are met (that happened outside) but that we have fellowship with God. We share what's in our hearts; he shares what's in his.

2. *Having our hearts sprinkled from an evil conscience.* This is the language of the ancient cleansing rituals where the

priest would sprinkle water and blood on the person needing cleansing (Leviticus 14: 51). We are cleansed by Jesus' blood. As we've seen above, poor consciences have no place in the presence of God. There is no sin here: God does not condemn us.

We are in a holy place, but the holiness of the Holy Spirit works a little differently from the holiness of Yahweh. In the ancient tabernacle, the presence of God was kept physically separate from the people behind a veil and also protected by all the laws of holiness that the priests and Levites kept.

The holiness that God works in us is separation from the world in a moral sense. We live freely among the world, enjoying everything God has made, but we're different; our attitudes and responses, guided and taught by the Holy Spirit will re-discover the image of God within us so that we will reflect Christ.

3. *Let us hold fast the confession of our hope without wavering.* This is about us testifying and sharing the love and grace of Christ, not in this case so that sinners can be saved but so that we can be strengthened, and God glorified. We are recharged, re-energised and re-filled with hope.

4. *Let us consider one another in order to stir up love and good works.* It is also about the church as the Body of Christ. We must encourage one another – and if there are any problems or difficulties between us, these must be fixed in the outer court in a spirit of forgiveness and reconciliation. As we worship, we are edified – built up and strengthened together.

We'll look at this in a lot more detail in the chapter on Spiritual Gifts.

As we worship in the Sanctuary, we are joining our voices with the whole of creation in singing *Holy, holy, holy to the Lord God almighty! The heaven and earth are full of his glory.*

Worship in the Sanctuary

Worship in the *outer court* is centred on Jesus' Cross both as a challenge and a door. From that challenge, worshippers either move forward into the sanctuary or remain outside.

In the *sanctuary* Jesus is the focus too; but here the emphasis is not on us, our sin, or our response to the cross, but on who Jesus is; the products of the cross, his glory and our cleansing.

The time is coming, Jesus told the Samaritan woman, *when the true worshippers of God will worship the Father in spirit and in truth* (John 4: 23). Leaving aside the imagery of the Tabernacle with its lamps, bread and incense, we need to move into a place of intimacy with God. He is a Spirit and we are worshipping him on his own terms in his own language.

Worship in the sanctuary is described by Paul in 1 Corinthians chapters 11-14, where he teaches in depth about the Breaking of Bread; the Body of Christ and spiritual gifts.

Our part

In the sanctuary, our words and songs are to be addressed to God. I don't think it's terribly important whether we are addressing God as Father, or as Jesus or in the Person of the Holy Spirit, but I believe that it should be characterised by address in the second person – that is to 'You'. (Good theology is to address the Father in the name of Jesus Christ through the power of the Holy Spirit – but if we're coming with the right attitude, no one will complain.) Misty Edwards sings:

> *I don't want to talk about You*
> *like You're not in the room*
> *I want to look right at You,*
> *I want to sing right to You.*
>
> (Misty Edwards – Dove's Eyes)

We are speaking to our Father who loves us. We shouldn't need a script; F.H. Allen wrote:

> *Within the veil:*
> *For only as thou gazest*
> *Upon the matchless beauty of His face*
> *Can'st thou become a living revelation*
> *Of His great heart of love, his untold grace.*

This song implies a response to what God is saying – but I want to draw attention to the word *gaze*. *Gazing* is not something we generally do nowadays. It requires concentration, detachment and a certain peace of mind and heart, but it's the word that sums up what we are doing as we worship in the Sanctuary. We are gazing on the matchless beauty of the face of Jesus Christ (2 Corinthians 4: 6).

In the outer court, people look at you strangely if you 'gaze', but in the sanctuary, they're all doing it too.

God's Part

Like all worship, worship in the sanctuary is a conversation. We testify, sing and speak of the glory of God. We approach him and declare his beauty and our love for him. God responds by confirming our faith through Spiritual gifts given for the edification – the *building together* – of the church.

We must expect our Father to speak to us words of 'edification' that will build us up. Note: in this environment of worship in the sanctuary God does not speak to reprimand or condemn. Here, as we have already said, we are drawing near with a true heart – with our hearts cleansed from an evil conscience.

Discussion 6

The Tabernacle and the people who worked in it were made and kept holy by elaborate rituals. This cannot be the same for us – yet the same principles must apply.

- How can we promote a reverent attitude as you approach worship?

- How can we promote a reverent attitude as the meeting closes?

How important do you think an explicit act of confession is to corporate worship?

Have you ever felt the tangible presence of God, or do you trust that God is present because he promised to be?

- How important is it to feel the presence of God?

How far does our worship depend on the building or place we are in?

What strategies do you use to push through blockages to your own worship?

Read Ephesians 1.

- How can we use this chapter to guide worship in the Holy Place?

How can we 'gaze upon the matchless beauty of his face'.

7. The Sanctuary (the Holy Place) part 2

> *But we all, with unveiled face, beholding as in a mirror the glory of the Lord, are being transformed into the same image from glory to glory, just as by the Spirit of the Lord.*
>
> *(2 Corinthians 3: 18)*

Imagine that you could stand in front of God and talk to him face to face. What would you say? What would you feel like? What would you see? What would he say to you? How would you respond?

On our journey into worship we have come from the outside, the *outer court*, where our mind is filled with the priorities and the emergencies of everyday life, past the place of sacrifice – the cross – where Jesus takes all our rubbish, all our sin and failure and we put on his righteousness before God (2 Corinthians 5: 21), and entered the <u>sanctuary</u> – the Holy Place – where we can pour out our love and gratitude to God and he speaks to us. Only those who are in Christ can come here.

In the ancient Tabernacle, there was a second room which was the most intimate place with God, the *Most Holy Place* – the 'Holy of Holies'. This was at the far end from the entrance and curtained off from the Sanctuary by a thick curtain or 'veil'. Only the High Priest could enter this place, once a year on the Day of Atonement (Hebrews 9: 7) to offer a sacrifice for the sin of the whole nation.

The amazing thing – the truly remarkable thing – is that when Jesus died, his death *destroyed the veil* (Matthew 27: 51; Hebrews 10: 20), removing the distinction between the Sanctuary and the Most Holy Place. If we are in Christ, we are in the immediate presence of God. We approach the veil to find that it has been removed.

Think about this: by Jesus' death we have been brought into the very presence of God. The Most Holy Place is right here! But there is more: it gets better.

A Temple for the Holy Spirit

The Body of Christ

> *Do you not know that you are the temple of God and that the Spirit of God dwells in you?*
>
> *(1 Corinthians 3: 16)*

I've already mentioned that the church – that is, us – is known as the Body of Christ. This means that Jesus himself lives in us and through us in the world. Another way of looking at it is to see that *we are the place where God lives on earth*. So, it's not as if we have to come to the Most Holy Place; we have to understand (and it requires a major shift in our thinking) that we are the Most Holy Place.

> *Now, therefore, you are ... members of the household of God, [20] having been built on the foundation of the apostles and prophets, Jesus Christ Himself being the chief cornerstone, [21] in*

> *whom the whole building, being fitted together, grows into a holy temple in the Lord, ²² in whom you also are being built together for a dwelling place of God in the Spirit.*
>
> *(Ephesians 2: 19-22)*

This is the miracle that God has done in building the church. He has taken every different sort of people; social classes, ethnicities, cultures and genders and brought us together into the household of Christ. But we're not looking back at where we've come from, we're understanding and celebrating what we have become. Jesus is our *chief cornerstone* – the rock on which we are built – and the structure of teaching is laid down in the words of the Apostles and Prophets. We are being built into a holy dwelling place for God.

> *You also, as living stones, are being built up a spiritual house, a holy priesthood, to offer up spiritual sacrifices acceptable to God through Jesus Christ.*
>
> *(1 Peter 2: 5)*

The image here is a bit like the Body of Christ in 1 Corinthians 12, which is explored more fully later, but instead of parts of a body, he describes us as 'living stones' built up into a temple, and we are also the priests who serve in the temple. What we do and what we are, are contained in the same image.

In the teaching about the ancient Tabernacle in Exodus, the priests – Aaron and his sons – had to be bathed and anointed with oil in a particular way to make them holy for God's work (the *anointing* was to commission them for this special job). All their clothing was especially designed and made along with the materials used to make the Tabernacle itself. It was all holy – dedicated – to God. In a way, the priests were part of the Tabernacle. This is why Peter says that we're being made into a *spiritual house* and a *holy priesthood* in the same sentence.

So, individually we are the holy place where God lives. This means that our lives, the decisions we make about what we do, our interests and even the way we think, have to come into alignment with what God says and thinks. The Holy Spirit does this in us.

Together, we are more than this. Each of us forms part of the structure that God is building: he builds us – *edifies* us – into his holy temple. As you can imagine, some of us don't quite fit, so the Holy Spirit, like a stonemason (a *wise master-builder*, 1 Corinthians 3: 10) has to trim bits off so that we can slot into place.

Relationships

> *Do not be unequally yoked together with unbelievers. For ... what communion has light with darkness?* [15] *... Or what part has a believer with an unbeliever?* [16] *And what agreement has the temple of God with idols? For you are the temple of the living God. As God has said: "I will dwell in them and walk among them. I will be their God, and they shall be my people."*

(2 Corinthians 6: 14-16)

(See also Leviticus 26: 12, *I will walk among you and be your God*; Jeremiah 32: 38, *They shall be My people, and I will be their God*; Ezekiel 37: 27, *My tabernacle also shall be with them...*)

> *... do you not know that your body is the temple of the Holy Spirit who is in you, whom you have from God, and you are not your own?*

(1 Corinthians 6: 19)

Since God is making us into his holy dwelling-place, it matters how we live; it matters what relationships we have. Sometimes people will look at us and see God, but sometimes we send mixed messages by what we do.

In effect Paul is saying: 'Don't partner with just anybody; your body is the temple of God – it doesn't belong to you anymore.' Our sometimes stupid and ignorant behaviour doesn't alter the fact that God lives inside us – but it will confuse people and make them doubt, and perhaps cause them to judge unwisely. And, of course, the Holy Spirit in our conscience will give us a hard time too.

If two horses are pulling an old-fashioned plough together, and one of them is a racehorse and the other a Shetland pony, there will never be a straight furrow. If we are planning to get married or go into business or form any other close relationship involving mutual trust and shared goals, we need to be careful who our partners are or we will end up following opposing visions; being 'unequally yoked'. If we go into business with or marry someone who doesn't believe, it won't stop us being the Temple of the Holy Spirit, but it will frustrate us as we try to live out a Christian life and confuse others who see us. It may also mean that the relationship will fail.

In Paul's teaching about marriage (for example in Ephesians 5: 22-33) he shows that marriage is an illustration of Christ's relationship with the church (see chapter 8). If one of the partners doesn't believe that, the marriage may not be valid because both partners don't fully understand the relationship. A contract can only be binding between two parties who both fully understand and agree to it.

Don't be unevenly matched – you are the temple of the living God! (Remember what we said in Chapter 3 about church leaders being the *husband of one wife*. God wants us to form stable, godly and fruitful relationships so that we can model what society should look like and also be a means to heal it when it's broken.)

We don't need to build a temple on earth. We don't need a beautiful building to meet in (though it might be convenient to have one). We don't need to go anywhere or do anything special or different. Simply being Christians – being in Christ – cleansed by his blood and occupied by his Spirit, makes us the holiest, most beautiful thing there has ever been on earth.

One Mediator: Christ
Priests in the Old Testament *intercede* between the people and God. They were like go-betweens, and the High

Priest was the go-between for the entire nation. If people wanted to come to God, they needed a sacrifice and they needed a priest. This is now obsolete; Jesus is the ultimate sacrifice and the ultimate priest. We stand before God on our own – and on Christ's – account.

> *There is one God, and one mediator between God and men, the man Christ Jesus.*
>
> *(1 Timothy 2: 5 KJV)*

In Jesus Christ, God made the only way for us to come to God. He *said I am the way ... no one comes to the Father except through Me* (John 14: 6), and he made the way himself by taking the punishment for our sin. We are in a position to point others to him. As Paul says, how will they know unless someone tells them (Romans 14: 10)? This is what Peter means when he says we are a priesthood.

Worship in the Presence of God

> *I am the vine, you are the branches. He who abides in Me, and I in him, bears much fruit; for without Me you can do nothing ... If you abide in Me, and My words abide in you, you will ask what you desire, and it shall be done for you. ⁸ By this My Father is glorified, that you bear much fruit; so you will be My disciples.*
>
> *(John 15: 5, 7, 8)*

In this well-known passage in John 15, Jesus describes himself as a vine: *I am the vine and you are the branches* (v.5). If you look at a vine, it's not like a tree. The 'trunk' seems to be made up of the branches twisted about each other until they separate out. When the branches that form the original stem are cut back, they send out new shoots – these are normally trained on wire trellises. It's a great image because it emphasises that we and Jesus are part of the same body: the *Body of Christ*, his holy temple, many parts making one whole. The Vine consists of its branches. This is an amazing thing for Jesus to have said. You cannot separate the Vine from its branches.

How does this happen? As we abide in him, his words abide in us.

Paul says in Colossians 3: 16a – *Let the word of Christ dwell in you richly in all wisdom*. We've seen before, especially in Isaiah 6 how when we are in the presence of God, he gives us his Word as a challenge; a commission. As we saw with Isaiah in his vision, it needs a response.

"Whom shall I send ... Go ..."

(Isaiah 6: 8, 9)

There are various ways in which God speaks to us as we worship together: we read his Word in the Bible, he also speaks to us through the spiritual gifts such as prophecy. But the main way for God to speak to us in our worship together is through preaching.

Do you have the gift of speaking? Then speak as though God himself were speaking through you.

(1 Peter 4: 11 NLT)

Those who speak in the church congregation speak as though God himself were speaking through them. Of course, he does! We are the temple of the living God – we should expect him to.

This has two implications. Firstly, those who speak must be aware that God will speak through them. Preaching is a *prophetic gift*; speakers must believe that they are speaking the words of God, and that God is using them to speak to his people.

Speaking in this way comes with some responsibility. If I'm urging people to stop sinning and I'm sinning myself, I'm going to be exposed as a hypocrite. But it's deeper than that; those who preach or teach have to understand and live out what they are saying. In Christianity, practice comes before theory.

Secondly, when we come together as a congregation, we must expect God to speak through the preacher and receive what he says. This has nothing to do with delivery, style or the speaker's personality. If I come to church asking God to speak to me, I can't get upset if the preacher says something that I find uncomfortable.

In the same way that the Most Holy place with the Ark and the presence of God was the centre of the ancient Israelite worshipping community, the preaching of the Word is the central focus of our worship together.

Everything else we do, in preparing and leading a worship service, leading our brothers and sisters in song or in responding to the word of God, must look to the Word of God.

Response

The work of the Holy Spirit is to make us holy. How does this work? For most of my Christian experience I assumed that it took place by a kind of spiritual osmosis – that the Holy Spirit living within would gradually permeate my mind and make me more like Jesus. Unconsciously.

To some extent, this does appear to happen. As God reveals himself to me, I'm 'amazed by grace' and 'overwhelmed by love'; I find myself wanting more of Jesus and therefore making some of the right choices. (The previous sentence shows at least the importance of singing the right songs.) But many Christians I meet seem to drift like hot-air balloons across the landscape, without any clear sense of direction, hoping for a soft landing 'in heaven', and I suppose I've done it myself from time to time.

The Bible is much more straight-forward, however. It says, in words we keep coming back to:

> *I beseech you therefore, brethren, by the mercies of God, that you present your bodies a living sacrifice, holy, acceptable to God, which is your reasonable service.* [2] *And do not be conformed to this world, but be transformed by the renewing*

> *of your mind, that you may prove what is that good and acceptable and perfect will of God.*
>
> *(Romans 12: 1, 2)*

'Presenting our bodies as a living sacrifice' is a deliberate act. It is to put down our own concerns and sacrifice ourselves. That sounds extreme – but it's the teaching of Jesus. He said, *If any man will come after me, let him deny himself, and take up his cross, and follow me* (Matthew 16: 24). When he said this, it wasn't obvious how he was going to die – but the cross was a familiar and horrid sight in the Roman world. It was part pillory, where offenders were held up to public ridicule and part gallows where the victim would die slowly. The Romans executed hundreds of thousands of people in this way.

To 'take up your cross' is to take responsibility for your sins and your failings and their consequences and take them to Jesus. He says *Come to Me, all you who labour and are heavy laden, and I will give you rest* (Matthew 11: 28). This is a kind of continual repentance. When we first come to Christ in the outer court of worship, we repent and turn from our sin, but the process continues as the Holy Spirit continues to speak to us – and we keep returning to the cross.

Paul writes about it often:

> *Set your mind on things above, not on things on the earth. 3 For you died, and your life is hidden with Christ in God.*
>
> *(Colossians 3: 2, 3)*

(See also Romans 6: 6; 8: 36; 2 Corinthians 4: 11; Galatians 2: 20; Colossians 2: 20.)

This is not something that happens accidentally.

The ancient Tabernacle was made in a particular way and out of special materials; it contained furniture – the lamps, the bread, the incense – that illustrated the greatness, power and love of God, and at the centre was the Ark where the Presence of Yahweh himself was; it contained the Ten Commandments, the Word of God.

Our worship works in a similar way. The Word of God is at its centre and everything else sets the scene for it, helping the people to receive what God is saying. We have to know what we are doing when we respond to God's Word; it has to be a conscious act. He has given us free will and expects us to exercise it. This is very important. It is our reasonable service.

Paul continues that we should *not be conformed to the world* but *transformed by the renewing of our minds*. We are holy in that we are different from the world while we are present within it; we are distinct. This happens because we have our minds renewed as we hear and respond to the word of God.

> *The law of the LORD is perfect, converting the soul.*
>
> *(Psalm 19: 7)*

How do we do this 'rational worship' and become transformed? How is our 'soul' converted? By opening ourselves up and feeding on the words that come from God, and by responding to them.

When God speaks there is always a challenge and a call to follow him in a deeper service, and just like Isaiah, our response is *Here I am, send me*.

Worship in the Most Holy Place is firstly coming to understand ourselves as the place where God lives. Secondly it is seeking to hear the voice of God so that we can respond to it. Jesus said, quoting Deuteronomy: *Man shall not live by bread alone but by every word that proceeds from the mouth of God* (Matthew 4: 4; Deuteronomy 8: 3).

When we worship on our own or with others we must expect to hear and respond to what God says.

Discussion 7

Imagine that you could stand in front of God and talk to him face to face.

- What would you say?
- What would he say to you?

Practical question:

- If only those who are in Christ can worship in the Holy Place, what happens if unbelievers are present?
- Is it okay for unbelievers to take communion?

Think of some words that speak to you of the immediate presence of God.

- Turn these into a meditation, perhaps in the style of a Taizé chant.
- Discuss ways in which scripture can be used to inform and direct the flow of worship.
- What is (or should be) the central focus of our worship?

8. Intimacy with God

As a bridegroom rejoices over the bride, so shall your God rejoice over you

(Isaiah 62: 5)

I am jealous for you with godly jealousy. For I have betrothed you to one husband, that I may present you as a chaste virgin to Christ

(2 Corinthians 11: 2)

We've looked at the Church as the Body of Christ; we've looked at the Church as the temple of the Holy Spirit. There's another image commonly used in Scripture to describe the people of God, one that's harder to visualise but deeply important to the way we understand who we are in Christ. *The Bride of Christ.*

This can be hard to understand; after all, a large number of us are male. How does it work? How can a man be a bride? Also, how can the Church be the Body and the Bride of Christ at the same time? These images can be confusing but beginning to understand them can help us to make sense of who we are before God and how we should worship him.

This is a very big subject and there isn't space here to do it proper justice, but I will give a brief introduction to what it means to be the Bride of Christ.

What is a bride?

A woman about to be married or very recently married (Shorter Oxford English Dictionary).

The word bride refers to a particular period in an ongoing relationship – the time surrounding marriage. Prior to this comes *betrothal*, when a couple are engaged to be married, and before that comes *courtship*, where a man and a woman choose each other. Perhaps this approach seems old-fashioned, but a formal contract of marriage is at the heart of both the New and Old Testament communities – and traditionally marriage has been regarded as one of the building blocks that society rests on. The New Testament does not forbid arranged marriage, but the understanding is that partners come together freely. Also, the Bible is clear that marriage is monogamous – one man, one woman – life-long and 'fruitful'. Part of the purpose of marriage is the bearing and raising of children.

So, a bride is someone who is chosen, prepared and finally contracted (by vows, promises and usually a symbolic exchange like a dowry or a ring) to join a permanent and exclusive partnership with another.

A bride has a particular story, which will involve a move away from her parents' home to join her future husband (for example Genesis 24: 57-67 – Rebekah; Luke 2: 4, 5 – Mary).

The Bride's counterpart is the *bridegroom* – her husband – his story also involves leaving his parents and 'cleaving' (or being joined) to his wife (Genesis 2: 24; Ephesians 5: 31).

Marriage is defined slightly differently in different cultures, and incorporates cultural and legal obligations, as well as Scriptural teaching – but the biggest thing that defines this relationship is love.

Marriage

(Note that this section relates to marriage between Christians in the context of the church.)

Everybody thinks they know what marriage is and this leads to some confusion in debate, but the Bible teaches that marriage is the basic relationship between men and women; it also teaches that it is a picture of Christ and the church.

> *Therefore a man shall leave his father and mother and be joined to his wife, and they shall become one flesh.*
>
> *(Genesis 2: 24)*

The word 'sex' comes from the Latin word *secus*, meaning 'division', that is, the division of living things into male and female. This verse from Genesis describes in some sense the healing of this division, where the man and the woman come together to form a single unit. In Genesis 1: 27, 28, we are told that God made the man and the woman *together* in his own image – so that in some way they reflect his nature.

This shows us that *relationship* is part of God's character. He teaches us to know him by being in fellowship together; the unity of a man and a woman, male and female helps us to understand God. *It is not good for the man to be alone* (Genesis 1: 18).

In the beginning of Genesis God makes his creation orderly and fruitful; his first command to the man and the woman was to *be fruitful and multiply* along with the rest of creation.

Notice that creation is gendered; it is fertile and fruitful and procreates sexually. Much of the Bible is about things being fruitful – the land is fertile; family groups, nations and races multiply and grow; farmers sow and reap; the influence of the Holy Spirit in people's lives is described as *fruit*, and the gospel message itself is described as *seed*.

The coming together of the man and the woman is about:

Fulfilment: The man was alone and now he's together; before he was a divided half, now he's whole. The writer Philip Yancey[9] describes how the existence of romantic love led him to rediscover his faith in God. This coming together and the fulfilment sought in the 'healing' of the division between men and women is the essence of romantic love.

A family unit or household: A man leaves his father and mother and joins his wife; elsewhere women leave their family situations and join their husbands. The stable household is at the heart of God's Law for ancient Israel, and respect for family is what has kept the Jewish identity alive for the two thousand years since the Diaspora.

In a similar way the family household is at the heart of the early church.

Being fruitful' – in other words, raising children, and so procreating the human race.

Paul's teaching on marriage is hard to understand in the 21st century; it was probably hard to understand in the 1st century too. He describes it in spiritual terms in this key passage from his Letter to the Ephesians.

> *Husbands, love your wives, just as Christ also loved the church and gave Himself for her, [26] that He might sanctify and cleanse her with the washing of water by the word, [27] that He might present her to Himself a glorious church, not having spot or wrinkle or any such thing, but that she should be holy and without blemish. [28] So husbands ought to love their own wives as their own bodies; he who loves his wife loves himself. [29] For no one ever hated his own flesh, but nourishes and cherishes it, just as the Lord does the church. [30] For we are members of His body, of His flesh and of His bones. [31] "For this reason a man shall leave his father and mother and be joined to his wife, and the two shall become one flesh." [32] This is a great mystery, but I speak concerning Christ and the church. [33] Nevertheless let each one of you in particular*

> *so love his own wife as himself, and let the
> wife see that she respects her husband.*
>
> *(Ephesians 5: 25-33)*

The central point in this passage is that the husband represents Christ; the purpose of the passage is to illustrate the relationship between Christ and the church, not to offer relationship guidance. Our problem in reading this is that we don't really understand the idea of Christ as a *bridegroom* and ourselves as a *bride*. Paul isn't telling us that the relationship between Christ and the church is a *bit like* a marriage; he's saying that marriage is a picture of Christ and the church. The coming together of a man and a woman in marriage bears witness to a deeper and eternal truth.

This is why adultery and divorce are such a big deal in the Bible – the command against adultery is next to the command against murder (Exodus 20: 13, 14). They dissolve a union that is basic to how God has made us and that is also at the heart of how we understand his relationship with us. Sylvia Mary Alison writes[10]:

> *I had a visual impression of the husband and wife
> as one flesh, one entity, and as they got divorced
> it looked like an amputation, the body was sawn
> in two and the limbs left quivering and bleeding.*

A striking image. God says that he hates divorce (Malachi 2: 16 NLT): *To divorce your wife is to overwhelm her with cruelty … so guard your heart; do not be unfaithful to your wife.* This is not to judge or condemn those who have suffered divorce, but rather to grieve with them the lasting hurt that has been caused.

One of the fundamental relationships in all of Creation – perhaps the most fundamental – is God's relationship with humankind. The story of the Bible is the story of this relationship that begins with the union of a man and a woman in the Garden but a separation from God and ends with the *marriage of the Lamb* in Revelation 19. Courtship and marriage is basic to the experience of being human (certainly in Biblical terms); it's also basic to being godly: God courts us and we respond.

The Divine Romance
– Images in the Song of Solomon

> *For your Maker is your husband, The LORD of hosts is His name*
>
> *(Isaiah 54: 5)*

The Song of Solomon is a love poem describing a romance between a man (an aristocrat or prince in Jerusalem) and a young woman, described as a *Shulamite*, meaning that she came from Shulam. Women from Shulam were supposed to be very beautiful.

She begins:

> *Let him kiss me with the kisses of his mouth—for your love is better than wine.* [3] *Because of the fragrance of your good ointments, your name is ointment poured forth...*
>
> *(Song 1: 2, 3)*

He responds a little later:

> *I have compared you, my love, to my filly among Pharaoh's chariots.* ¹⁰ *Your cheeks are lovely with ornaments, your neck with chains of gold.*
>
> *(Song. 1: 9, 10)*

The language is rich, poetic and sensual. We might find some of the images odd – but remember that it's probably 3,000 years old. Below, I'll discuss a couple of these images in detail.

1: The Passionate Lover

From the last chapter of the book:

> *(The Woman's relatives):*
>
> *Who is this coming up from the wilderness, leaning upon her beloved? …*
>
> *(Song. 8: 5)*

The image is of the woman and her lover-husband coming up out of the desert; she is leaning on his shoulder. This passage follows a description of them lying together in an amorous embrace (she is entwined in his arms while he sleeps); clearly, they have been enjoying one-another's intimate company, and now they are returning together. I am reminded of Hosea 2: 14-17. Hosea was a prophet to Israel who was told to marry a promiscuous woman called Gomer in the full knowledge that she would be unfaithful to him. This demonstrated the way in which the people of Israel continually broke the Covenant they had with Yahweh in a kind of spiritual adultery. But just as God was gracious to Israel, Hosea would be gracious to Gomer. He will try to win her if it's possible.

In Chapter 2: 1-13 Hosea explains that unless Gomer (that is, Israel) *puts away the adulterous look from her face and the unfaithfulness from between her breasts* (v.2 NIV) he will expose her infidelity publicly and she will be ruined; he will also reject her children and oppose her every step as she chases after her lovers (vv. 4-8).

But then he says:

> *"Therefore, behold, I will allure her, will bring her into the wilderness, and speak comfort to her. [15] I will give her ... the Valley of Achor [suffering] as a door of hope; she shall sing there, as in the days of her youth ...*
>
> [16] *"And it shall be, in that day," says the* LORD, *"That you will call Me 'My Husband,' and no longer call Me 'My Master,'* [17] *for I will take from her mouth the names of the [false gods], and they shall be remembered by their name no more.*
>
> (Hosea 2: 14-17)

This is speaking at the same time to Gomer and to the nation of ancient Israel. Here is an image of God as a suitor, a passionate husband, drawing his unfaithful Bride into a quiet place almost by deception (*alluring* her), so that he can 'speak comfort to her'. He will court her and make her love him, then he will turn her suffering into hope and the optimistic dreams of her childhood will be restored; she will no longer call him 'master' but 'husband'.

In the light of this, the image of the Shulamite woman in Song of Solomon 8 coming out of the wilderness *leaning on her beloved* after a night of intimacy takes on a new perspective. This is what Hosea wants Gomer to do, to lean on him, not just in dependency but to be satisfied with his love. To the people of Israel, Yahweh presented himself as a jealous lover, not because he was demanding submission or demonstrating his power but because he was a protective and passionate husband. This is not the way we usually think of God in the Old Testament.

We find the same image is in the New Testament too. John the Baptist says of Jesus:

> *He who has the bride is the bridegroom; but the friend of the bridegroom, who stands and hears him, rejoices greatly because of the bridegroom's voice. Therefore this joy of mine is fulfilled.*

(John 3: 29)

The 'bride', once again, is the people of Israel, those who are hearing John's message at the time that Jesus is beginning his ministry, and Jesus is the 'bridegroom'. John portrays himself as the friend of the bridegroom – in other words, the 'best man' at the wedding; his role is to prepare the way for the bridegroom. Jesus picks this image up in Matthew 9: 15: *Can the friends of the bridegroom mourn as long as the bridegroom is with them?*

Paul uses the same language about the church and presents himself as a kind of best man in 2 Corinthians 11: 2:

> *I have betrothed you to one husband, that I may present you as a chaste virgin to Christ.*

This pattern of imagery finds its fulfilment in Revelation 19, where Jesus – referred to as the Lamb – is married:

> *Let us be glad and rejoice and give Him glory, for the marriage of the Lamb has come, and His wife has made herself ready.*
>
> *(Revelation 19: 7)*

Some readers say that 'the Bride' stands for Israel, not the church. I disagree. In the Old Testament Israel is sometimes referred to as a bride and Yahweh as her husband, and Jesus referred to himself as the bridegroom, partially fulfilling this. As we have seen, this is completely fulfilled in Revelation 19 at the marriage of the Lamb (v.17: *his wife has made herself ready*). This refers to the church, whom Paul has (in his own words) betrothed to Christ.

It is impossible to separate the Bride in the Old Testament from the Bride in the New Testament. Christ – the Lamb of God – only has one wife.

2. *Spikenard*

> *While the king is at his table, my spikenard sends forth its fragrance.*

> *[13] A bundle of myrrh is my beloved to me, [he shall] lie all night between my breasts.*

(Song. 1: 12, 13)

Spikenard is an aromatic oil used in the making of incense and as a perfume; it has a sweet and distinctive aroma. It was one of the ingredients that made up the holy incense used on the altar in the Tabernacle, but here it is used as a perfume. In those days, it was found only in a few valleys high in the Himalayas, so it was rare and very costly. It is mentioned a couple of times in Song of Solomon, where it shows a promise of romantic intimacy.

> *A garden enclosed is my sister, my spouse,*
> *A spring shut up, a fountain sealed.*
>
> *[13] Your plants are an orchard of pomegranates*
> *With pleasant fruits, fragrant henna with*
> *spikenard,*
>
> *[14] Spikenard and saffron, calamus and cinnamon,*
> *With all trees of frankincense,*
> *Myrrh and aloes, with all the chief spices—*
>
> *[15] A fountain of gardens, a well of living waters,*
> *And streams from Lebanon.*
>
> *[16] Awake, O north wind, and come, O south!*
> *Blow upon my garden, that its spices may flow out.*
> *Let my beloved come to his garden*
> *And eat its pleasant fruits.*
>
> *(Song. 4: 12-16)*

In Song of Solomon 4 the man says, as part of a fine description of her beauty and his passionate and sensuous responses to her, *you have ravished my heart with one look of your eyes* (v.9). Then in this second section he describes his lover as *a garden enclosed* (v.12) with fruit and beautiful fragrances, an image full of mystery and anticipation. She is closed to him at the moment, but he is aware – acutely aware – of what is hidden inside, the rich fruit, spices and perfumes. He makes a long list of all the exotic things he can think of, that might be inside, spikenard among them.

The woman responds (v.16) by calling on the winds to blow so that the perfume will flow out, enticing him even more; inviting him to come and enter this private and secluded space and share its fruit.

In the Song of Solomon, spikenard is associated with deep intimacies eagerly anticipated by both partners.

The next time we see Spikenard oil is in John 12. Jesus is in Bethany at the house of Lazarus, whom Jesus raised from the dead:

> *Then Mary took a pound of very costly oil of spikenard, anointed the feet of Jesus, and wiped His feet with her hair. And the house was filled with the fragrance of the oil.*

(John 12: 3)

Mary and Martha were Lazarus' sisters. We first meet them in Luke 10: 38-41, where Martha invites Jesus to stay at their house; she is very busy looking after her guests and complains to Jesus about Mary who is listening to him rather than helping her. He tells her that Mary has *chosen the better part*.

Then in John 11, when Lazarus dies, it is Martha again who meets Jesus and speaks to him; Mary is sitting in the house, overwhelmed by grief. After Lazarus' resurrection, Mary, Martha, Lazarus, Jesus and his disciples dine together. Martha is serving again when Mary anoints Jesus' feet with expensive spikenard oil and wipes them with her hair. *The house was filled with the fragrance of the oil.*

In doing what she does, she says that all her affections – her love, her desire and her possessions – belong to Jesus. She loves him completely and without holding anything back. This is an act of worship, and the fragrance filling the house is like the incense filling the Tabernacle. This is discussed more fully in Chapter 13.

Spikenard oil was an exotic perfume and its use implies intimacy and desire; it was also used in worship and the fragrance filling the house reminds us of the rich incense filling the Tabernacle.

Lessons for us in worship

We are the Bride of Christ as well as his Body (Ephesians 5: 30, 31). This is not just a legal status or a poetic image, but the spiritual union described by Paul in Ephesians. As we follow the pattern through the Scriptures, it becomes clear that being a bridegroom – a suitor and a husband – is part of God's eternal nature. He says in Jeremiah 31: 3: *I have loved you with an everlasting love;*

therefore with loving-kindness I have drawn you. In Jesus' death on the cross he has demonstrated his love for us by laying his life down to rescue us from death so that he can be united with us at last.

Like Hosea, trying to win his wayward wife so that she'll be more like the Shulamite woman in the Song of Solomon, God wants us to be in love with him; he wants to be our preoccupation and the object of our desire. This is the meaning of the First and Great Commandment (Matthew 22: 38). Like Mary, he wants us to give our whole heart to him extravagantly and without reservation – even if other people think we're crazy or wrong.

Think of the passage in Song of Solomon 4 again, but this time with Jesus as the man and ourselves as the woman – we are the *garden enclosed*, full of exotic spices and fruit. He is enchanted with our beauty and full of anticipation. Is it possible for us to read Song of Solomon 4 and see ourselves as the one loved? It sounds wrong – irreverent, even – but this is nevertheless what God is saying to us.

But we are so often like Hosea's Gomer, our attention span for Spiritual things is tiny and we are easily distracted. Yet he loves us with the passion that created Niagara Falls and the Whirlpool Galaxy, and with the love that took Jesus to the cross. His desire for us is that we will love him; to come up from our wilderness leaning on our beloved.

> *Thy renown went forth among the heathen for thy beauty: for it was perfect*

> *through my comeliness, which I had put upon thee, saith the LORD God.*

(Ezekiel 16: 14 KJV)

It's hard to see ourselves in this way – probably impossible while we live on earth. But when we worship in the presence of God – in the holy place – we are like the woman asking the winds to blow upon the garden so that the fragrance, the beauty *that he has put upon us*, will flow out. It is the Holy Spirit who blows into us, not so that we can be blessed or 'filled', but so that Jesus – our bridegroom, our lover – can enjoy our companionship and worship.

> *The LORD thy God in the midst of thee is mighty; he will save, he will rejoice over thee with joy; he will rest in his love, he will joy over thee with singing.*

(Zephaniah 3: 17 KJV)

In our Free Church culture, we sometimes make 'spiritual love' a very high, holy and cold thing. We sharply define it against other kinds of love that are inferior. *Love* that *lays its life down for its friends*. But I believe that God wants us to know the *fulness* of love in Christ. Spiritual love must include the rich friendship that David had with Jonathan and Jesus had with Lazarus, Mary and Martha; it must include Mary's outright passion and Peter's determination to follow him no matter what. It must include the insights that John – the disciple whom Jesus loved – brings us, but for us first and foremost it is something that we must cultivate in ourselves for him with the help of the Holy Spirit.

When we worship in the holy place, Jesus is our focus and passion. Our purpose is not to be satisfied, to have our doubts resolved or to fulfil a religious duty, it is to delight him. He is our single audience; he says to us: *you have dove's eyes behind your veil.* Let us return his gaze with adoration.

> *A glimpse of God will save you. To gaze at him will [make you holy].*
>
> (Manley Beasley)

Discussion 8

In what sense are we the Bride of Christ?

Your name is as ointment poured forth.

- How does this phrase apply to worship in the church?

The songs we sing form much of our spiritual and theological vocabulary, yet there is a genre of worship songs that are almost indistinguishable from romantic pop songs.

- Is this appropriate?
- How can we express intimacy with God as his Bride, and not make it sound awkward?

Consider the song 'Above all Power' (Paul Baloche and Lenny LeBlanc).

- Read it carefully line by line:
- How would you use this song to help worship?
- Do you agree with how the song describes God?
- Is it possible to use songs when you're not sure about the theology they express?

9. The Power of Praise

If we lose the war in the air, we lose the war and lose it quickly

(Field Marshal Bernard Montgomery).

...command of the air is of first priority to any military success in war

(Dale O. Smith).

... the prince of the power of the air, the spirit who now works in the sons of disobedience.

(Ephesians 2: 2 KJV).

You've heard of the Salvation Army: the power of praise is the air force. When we praise God; when we declare his majesty, speaking and singing the truth about him in love, the spiritual world around us pays attention. The angels rejoice because we are joining our voices to theirs; the demons cringe; their strongholds are shaken.

In a dark and difficult situation, when the earth seems *formless and void*, singing the praise of God is like saying *let there be light*. Declaring God's praise works with prayer as a lever to shift obstacles to the gospel.

At War

The Bible is rich with military imagery. Some people nowadays are uncomfortable with this, but it is very much part of Scripture. In the Old Testament, the promise to Abraham consisted in part of a piece of land;

this was realised in the time of Joshua (a warrior) – the books of Joshua and Judges tell of the battles fought to establish the nation of Israel in its promised home – and came to maturity under David (a warrior king) and Solomon. Later the kingdoms of Judah and Israel were threatened by the empires of Assyria and Babylon and more battles were fought, this time with a very definite spiritual dimension as kings like Jehoshaphat and Hezekiah demonstrated their trust in God, while Ahab and Zedekiah showed that their trust was elsewhere.

The security of the land was directly related to the people's spiritual welfare; when they rejected God's Covenant they were invaded and taken into exile.

In the New Testament, the military language might be less fundamental to the message, but it's still important, for example:

- in Matthew 10: 34, Jesus says that he brings *not peace but a sword*;

- in Romans 12: 13: Paul speaks of the *armour of light*; again in 2 Corinthians 6: 7 Paul mentions the armour of righteousness, and

- in 2 Corinthians 10: 4, 5 he says: *the weapons of our warfare are ... mighty in God for pulling down strongholds*.

The best-known military passage is in Ephesians 6: 10-20 where Paul describes in detail the whole armour of God needed for protection in spiritual conflict.

The presence of the Roman military was very much part of life in the first century, both as an occupying force and as protectors of the general peace. In Paul's letters Epaphroditus, Timothy and Archippus are all called 'fellow-soldiers' (Philippians 2: 25; 2 Timothy 2: 3 and Philemon 2). Paul uses the picture of military conflict to promote obedience to God's authority and strong self-discipline; to show how the Holy Spirit's protection works like armour, and to illustrate the spiritual struggle that we must all undertake every day with the forces of darkness. This is shown clearly in the life of Jesus and the early Christians.

As Christians, we are in a constant state of warfare, whether we see it or not. It's not fought out in physical battles (Jesus said that his kingdom is not of this world), but in a Spiritual dimension that we don't have access to through our natural understanding. *Your adversary, the Devil*, says Peter (1 Peter 5: 8) *walks about like a roaring lion, seeking whom he may devour*. We must be constantly vigilant; constantly on guard, but confident in the protection of the Holy Spirit and Christ's ultimate victory at the cross.

In the past and even today in some places, Christians have tried to take out their differences with each other in physical conflict – in intimidation, persecution and violence. This is completely to misunderstand both the gospel and the nature of the Christian faith. It is never about power and territory: *the weapons of our warfare are not carnal*, says Paul. We cannot fight to defend the truth: the truth defends us.

'Binding the Strong Man'

> *Then one was brought to Him who was demon-possessed, blind and mute; and He healed him, so that the blind and mute man both spoke and saw.* ²³ *And all the multitudes were amazed and said, "Could this be the Son of David?"*
>
> ²⁴ *Now when the Pharisees heard it they said, "This fellow does not cast out demons except by Beelzebub, the ruler of the demons."*
>
> ²⁵ *But Jesus knew their thoughts, and said to them: "Every kingdom divided against itself is brought to desolation, and every city or house divided against itself will not stand.* ²⁶ *If Satan casts out Satan, he is divided against himself. How then will his kingdom stand?* ²⁷ *And if I cast out demons by Beelzebub, by whom do your sons cast them out? Therefore they shall be your judges.* ²⁸ *But if I cast out demons by the Spirit of God, surely the kingdom of God has come upon you.* ²⁹ *Or how can one enter a strong man's house and plunder his goods, unless he first binds the strong man? And then he will plunder his house.*
>
> *(Matthew 12: 22-29)*

In this passage Jesus heals a demon-possessed man and the Pharisees – the religious scholars of the day – comment that *This fellow does not cast out demons except by*

Beelzebub, the ruler of the demons. They claimed that he only had power over demons because he was himself the chief devil. Jesus responded with the picture of a civil war: if Satan fights against Satan (v.26), his kingdom will fall.

This also gives us a rather uncomfortable image of the Devil[11], Satan, being the ruler of a kingdom with structure, integrity and strength. We don't like to consider this too closely, but it ties in with what the Bible says elsewhere about *strongholds, principalities* and *powers*. Satan's kingdom is not a random association of 'badness', according to Jesus – it's organised. We are not going to oppose it successfully unless we are organised too – that is, unless we take our places under Christ, our head.

It may be that you are sceptical about the 'kingdom of darkness' and see it as medieval superstition, but the Bible gives a coherent and compelling picture of the spiritual environment. Perhaps you want to read spiritual conflict as metaphorical or symbolic of something else; it's possible to do this, but in any case, if we are serious about seeing the power of God transforming lives, we have to read the Bible in its own terms. We can't ignore the words of Jesus and the Apostles because they seem old-fashioned or quaint.

Jesus continued:

> *... how can one enter a strong man's house and plunder his goods, unless he first binds the strong man? (v. 29).*

Jesus wasn't advocating burglary – but part of his commission foretold by Isaiah (Isaiah 61: 1) is *to proclaim liberty to the captives and the opening of the prison to those who are bound.* We want to win men and women to Christ; to lead them out of darkness and into his light; ultimately, we want to see them become disciples of Jesus and to live fruitful and worthy lives. In order to do this, we must bind the strong man who holds them.

When we preach the gospel and declare the kingdom of God, we engage in conflict with powers we can't see and can hardly imagine. If this sounds scary, it should do. When we do evangelism in a prison for example, it's very easy to imagine a stronghold – a prison is a physical *stronghold.* But everywhere hearts and minds – souls – are being kept in similar conditions. Like Paul and Silas in Philippi (see below) we need the Holy Spirit's intervention to be successful.

We have already discussed how the Word of God challenges and changes us in worship. As we lead worship, we need to help the congregation to be ready to hear and respond to what God is going to say to them. How can we bind the strong man through worship?

Order

If you were to walk into one of Her Majesty's prisons and attempt to release the legally convicted offenders inside, surprisingly quickly you would find yourself sharing their accommodation. In due course, these prisoners will be released after the correct procedures have been followed, a process which might take many years.

Something similar is likely to happen if we take it upon ourselves to proclaim liberty to spiritual captives; men and women are spiritually bound according to God's righteousness because they are sinners *[living] their lives as slaves to the fear of dying* (Hebrews 2: 15 NLT), and their fears are justified because without Christ they have no hope. When the sons of Sceva tried to cast out demons by Jesus whom Paul preaches (Acts 19: 11-20) they found their hands more than full and fled *naked and wounded*.

Our actions must be orderly. God wants all captives released, and Jesus, by dying on the cross has signed their pardon, yet they remain in the old stronghold and spiritual liberty and salvation can seem a long way off. They are held, in fact, by an *illusion*. In Acts 12 Peter was in prison and the prayers of his brothers and sisters released him. An angel came and guided him out of the stronghold, but Peter had to walk in faith in order to be free. The prison could no longer hold him, but doubt might have.

We must *bind the strong man* – and take very seriously the teaching of Paul about Spiritual armour, as well as learning lessons from the Old Testament heroes like Hezekiah and Daniel.

Spiritual Warfare

We don't have to go and fight the Devil directly because Jesus has done that for us – and his victory is complete. Ephesians 4: 8-10 tells us about Jesus' descent into the 'lower parts' and subsequently his ascent into heaven *leading captivity captive* (KJV), in other words, changing the circumstances of the people in captivity so that they are subject to his rule of love, like Peter and the angel. We move in Jesus' footsteps (we were once captives too and he set us free) not against the Devil but against the principalities and powers that have control in this world. Soldiers fighting in World War 2 might have said they were fighting against Hitler, but in fact they were fighting the panzer divisions and storm-troopers – the *principalities and powers* – that he deployed against them.

> *We do not wrestle against flesh and blood, but against principalities, against powers, against the rulers of the darkness of this age, against spiritual hosts of wickedness in the heavenly places.*

(Ephesians 6: 12)

We must not underestimate the Devil's power and influence. I get worried sometimes by Christians who declare that they are going to do battle with Satan. I'm reminded of Lewis Carroll's nonsense poem 'Jabberwocky': *He took his vorpal sword in hand, / Long time the manxome foe he sought.* We don't want to go charging off into the 'tulgey wood', waving our vorpal swords after an enemy we don't fully understand. This is dangerous: we must not *speak evil of dignities* (2 Peter 2: 10; Jude 8). Our place is to resist the Devil with a humble attitude (James 4: 6, 7) and to submit ourselves to God. The Devil will flee from us.

Principalities and Powers

Think of a place where all the people strongly believed something that is untrue, Communist Russia, for example, or Nazi Germany. The people lived under a police state – they were not able to speak or think freely and when individuals went against the ruling authorities they were often dealt with very harshly.

Most people live under a false idea of one kind or another; they cannot exercise true freedom because their minds have not been renewed. Even though Christ died for their sin, they still see the walls, fences and locks of their prison. People without the Holy Spirit have no power to change themselves spiritually; the natural human mind cannot be free from itself. So, it is impossible for us to bring people to Christ by force of persuasion or by making them feel good or excited, guilty or anything else. They are being held captive by forces that are stronger than they are; by a strong man who won't let them go easily.

As we lead worship in the outer court with praise and declaration of the truth, we create a space where people are able to believe and respond to the gospel; we make a place where Jesus is named as Lord and where God's way is the 'normal' way. This will loosen the grip of the enemy and make it possible for people to believe and respond to the message.

Airpower: Controlling the Environment

This chapter started off with some quotations about air power. The Devil is described as *the prince of the power of the air* because he controls the environment in most places most of the time. Today we have a rather different view of warfare from Paul's. While the equipment carried by a Roman soldier in those days was remarkably similar to what is carried by a modern soldier, a Roman soldier could not call down an air-strike on his opponents. He had to grapple it out hand-to-hand.

In modern warfare, we understand that the side that controls the airspace is likely to be victorious because it can control the environment of the battlefield. In 1940 the Nazi Germans put a great effort into breaking the British air defences before their planned invasion – an effort that failed.

In every spiritual activity, whether we are leading worship on a Sunday morning, or preparing to conduct an evangelistic mission, we must control the spiritual environment in order to lead others into the presence of God. This is done through praise in the outer court of worship – declaring the sovereignty and power of God – and through prayer.

Our Weapons

> *For though we walk in the flesh, we do not [make] war according to the flesh.* [4] *For the*

> *weapons of our warfare are not carnal but mighty in God for pulling down strongholds, ⁵ casting down arguments and every high thing that exalts itself against the knowledge of God, bringing every thought into captivity to the obedience of Christ.*

(2 Corinthians 10: 3-5)

Praise

Singing and declaring praise to God is a powerful way in which we can control the spiritual environment.

> *At midnight Paul and Silas were praying and singing hymns to God, and the prisoners were listening to them ²⁶ Suddenly there was a great earthquake ... and immediately all the doors were opened and everyone's chains were loosed. ²⁷ And the keeper of the prison, awaking from sleep and seeing the prison doors open ... was about to kill himself. ²⁸ But Paul called with a loud voice, saying, "Do yourself no harm, for we are all here."*
>
> *²⁹ Then he called for a light, ran in, and fell down trembling before Paul and Silas. ³⁰ And he brought them out and said, "Sirs, what must I do to be saved?"*

(Acts 16: 25-29)

When Paul and Silas were arrested in Philippi, they were beaten and put into the inner dungeon of the prison with their feet in stocks. Their response, in spite of their desperate situation, was to sing praise to God. The result was that not only they, but all the other prisoners were released, and the jailer and his family were saved. This is an example of the presence of God in praise breaking a literal stronghold.

Of course, Paul and Silas weren't there by choice; they were forced into a situation where all they had at their disposal was praise.

When Jehoshaphat, King of Judah, had to defend himself against the Ammonites, he used what must have seemed an unusual military tactic:

> ... *And when he had consulted with the people, he appointed those who should sing to the LORD, and who should praise the beauty of holiness, as they went out before the army and were saying: "Praise the LORD, for His mercy endures forever."*
>
> [22] *Now when they began to sing and to praise, the LORD set ambushes against the people of Ammon, Moab, and Mount Seir, who had come against Judah; and they were defeated.*
>
> (2 Chronicles 20: 21, 22)

So, the choir was sent out in the front rank of the army. When we praise God from the heart, we render him present and our enemy has no foothold. In fact, what Jehoshaphat did was to use 'air power' to control the environment of the battle ... and they did not need to fight. When we praise God in that way, we turn whatever place we are in into the court of heaven. This is why Jesus taught us to pray *may your Kingdom come soon; may your will be done on earth as it is in heaven,* immediately after *Our Father in heaven may your name be kept holy* (Matthew 6: 9, 10).

Prayer: supplication
In other words, 'asking for things':

> *Be careful for nothing; but in every thing by prayer and supplication with thanksgiving let your requests be made known unto God...*
>
> *(Philippians 4: 6)*

We must ask God for what we need specifically and explicitly in the grateful knowledge that he *will supply all [our] needs according to his riches...* (v. 19). We are seeking to lead people in worship, so we can be sure that we are acting in God's will, so we can be confident in faith. We must keep a sense of perspective; sometimes we are asking God for things that seem impossible, but we have to remember who he is and that nothing is impossible with him. We can be thankful for the things we have already received and for the things that God is going to do.

One of the ways the enemy can resist us is to undermine our confidence or create blockages – that's why Paul often tells us to be orderly and disciplined in our prayer – the following verse is the natural result:

> ... and the peace of God, which [passes] all understanding, shall keep your hearts and minds through Christ Jesus.
>
> (Philippians 4: 7)

Prayer: intercession

> Pray in the Spirit at all times and on every occasion. Stay alert and be persistent in your prayers for all believers everywhere. And pray for me [Paul], too.
>
> (Ephesians 6: 18, 19 NLT)

Intercession is praying for other people.

In Exodus 17 Moses stands on a hill overlooking Israel's battle with the Amalekites and raises his staff in the air – this gives the Israelites success. As he becomes tired, Aaron and Hur support his arms (Exodus 17: 8ff). This is intercession in action: when we are tired, our Christian friends and our colleagues can rally to our support.

Intercessory prayer is an application of the *whole armour* described by Paul in Ephesians 6. We tend to think of the soldier in his armour standing on his own, but then – as now – that only happened when things went wrong. As the film *Gladiator* shows, the Roman soldier's armour wasn't designed for use in single combat but in the context of a fighting unit. The Roman army – like modern armies – manoeuvred in groups.

(The gladiators' equipment would have been rather different.)

Earlier in this chapter I referred to an illusion that holds people in bondage. We are also vulnerable to this, it is powerful and dangerous. Many people in evangelistic and pastoral ministries suffer from stress-related illnesses (as well as more direct opposition that can be easier to spot) that can remove them from ministry temporarily or permanently. Of course, it shouldn't happen, but nevertheless it does.

Roman shields (*shield of faith*, v. 16) were designed to interlock so that they formed a wall – each man's shield protected his left side and also the right side of the man next to him, so they had to stay close and be disciplined. We too need to stand together in faith – and support one another in prayer; in intercession.

We must also pray for the congregation as we prepare and during the worship time, especially for unbelievers who will be present so that Christ will be revealed to them. You may find it helpful to pray around the room or over each seat before the event or meeting begins as a way of bringing those who will be present before our Father – though of course, the seats themselves have no significance!

Discipline

> *Finally, my brethren, be strong in the Lord and in the power of His might.* [11] *Put on the whole armour of God, that you may be able to stand against the wiles of the devil.* [12] *For we do not*

> *wrestle against flesh and blood, but against principalities, against powers, against the rulers of the darkness of this age, against spiritual hosts of wickedness in the heavenly places.*
> *[13] Therefore take up the whole armour of God, that you may be able to withstand in the evil day, and having done all, to stand.*
>
> *[14] Stand therefore, having girded your waist with truth, having put on the breastplate of righteousness, [15] and having shod your feet with the preparation of the gospel of peace;[16] above all, taking the shield of faith with which you will be able to quench all the fiery darts of the wicked one. [17] And take the helmet of salvation, and the sword of the Spirit, which is the word of God; [18] praying always with all prayer and supplication in the Spirit, being watchful to this end with all perseverance and supplication for all the saints*
>
> (Ephesians 6: 10-18)

The word 'stand' is used four times in the first four verses. If a soldier under orders and under fire turns and runs, much damage is done. People may be hurt, not least the one who's running. The prophet Habbakuk says in Habbakuk 2: 1: *I will stand my watch and set myself on the rampart.* We must hold our ground.

Going back to 'Jabberwocky' and chasing monsters with our vorpal swords – it is more important to stand firm and hold ground than to seek conflict. This is the teaching of Paul in Ephesians 5. Towards the end of the second world war, much damage was caused to the Nazi regime by the allies' air-power, but in the end, it was British, Commonwealth, Soviet and American boots on the ground that won the war, their feet, as it were, *shod with the preparation of the gospel of peace.*

We know the truth: that Jesus is Lord and that he comes to seek and to save what is lost; we know our objective: to lead people to a place where they can be transformed by the Word of God. We may have feelings of inadequacy or unrighteousness; but we are cleansed by the blood of Jesus and no one can bring any accusation against the people God has chosen. If the atmosphere in the room is tending towards doubt, disruption or distortion, we have the authority to control the spiritual environment by declaring God's praise so that others can join in.

This is where we stand.

Fasting

We are not instructed to fast but fasting is often associated with spiritual maturity and discipline. The early church in the Acts fasted before they made important decisions (for example in Acts 13: 2 and 14: 23); fasting is also linked with prayer (Luke 2: 37). Fasting shifts our focus from the things of this world onto God; it reinforces our understanding that we have to trust him for all our provision. It is a way to demonstrate to God, and – perhaps more importantly – to ourselves, that we are serious about our relationship with him. It can help us gain clarity and perspective in spiritual matters and to renew our reliance upon God.

After Jesus' disciples failed to cast a demon out of a young man in Matthew 17, he said that power in prayer and authority over some demons at least came through *prayer and fasting* (v. 21 – although some modern translations omit 'fasting' from this).

Fasting will not make us any more saved, 'spiritual' or sanctified, but it will help us to be more focused and open to the Holy Spirit's direction and therefore more effective servants.

Summary

In this chapter, we've looked at how it is important to control the environment in which worship takes place so that people can be open to receive the word of God and respond to it. We described it as being like air power in modern warfare – where control of the air is critical to success.

As leaders in worship we seek to prepare the way for the Word of God. We do this by lifting up the name of Jesus Christ and emphasising his victory over sin at the cross. This takes the people's minds away from their perceived prison, the doubts, fears and dangers that surround them, and refocuses them on hope, freedom and salvation in Christ.

But this is a spiritual struggle. The darkness in people's hearts is not simple ignorance but belief in a lie that is backed up by demonic spiritual authority (2

Thessalonians 2: 11). We must be wise and well-prepared to come against this.

Nevertheless, the Name of Jesus is the supreme authority in all creation – and he binds the strong man. As we hold firm to truth and proclaim the gospel, we will see the power of God revealed.

Discussion 9

How comfortable do you feel with military imagery?

Discuss:

- In a worship service, how can we take control of the spiritual environment?
- Why would we do this?

Research:

Spend some time listening to the International House of Prayer 'Prayer Room' (they have a 24/7 web stream: (https://www.ihopkc.org/prayerroom/).

- How do they handle intercession and supplication?
- Suggest ideas for leading 'all kinds of prayer' in a worship service.

How does Paul's picture of the 'whole armour' of God (Ephesians 6: 10-20) guide our prayer and our worship generally?

- How do you understand the word 'stand' in this passage?

10. Using the Bible, Songs and Testimony

Preparation

> *Scripture should have a central place in our worship, for it is in and through Scripture that God speaks to us afresh the word of forgiveness and hope which is fully revealed ... in Jesus Christ.*
>
> *(Ellis, 2009, p.104)*

As we have noted before, the purpose of leading worship is to bring the people to a place where God can speak to them and they can receive what he says. In this way, the Body of Christ will be built strongly on its proper foundation – Christ.

So, the place to start preparation for leading worship is always with the Word of God. Christ is the Word of God and he – his words, his character and his presence – are revealed in Scripture; in the Bible:

> *In the beginning was the Word, and the Word was with God, and the Word was God. 2 He was in the beginning with God.*
>
> *(John 1: 1, 2)*

> *And the Word became flesh and dwelt among us, and we beheld His glory, the glory as of the only begotten of the Father.*
>
> *(John 1: 14)*

> *Sanctify them by Your truth. Your word is truth.*
>
> *(John 17: 17)*

How we achieve this is a personal thing that comes out of our own fellowship with God, but in this Chapter, I'll share some thoughts and ideas that might be helpful. How we select the particular readings we use will vary. They might be related to a programme of teaching or ministry that the whole church is undertaking; they might be part of our own on-going conversation with the Holy Spirit, or they could be based in our personal study or meditation. Sometimes – rarely, I think – the Holy Spirit will give something completely different. And just as our individual relationship with God is based on Biblical truth, this is equally important for the congregation as a whole. The church must be guided by Scripture.

Our own preferences, our thoughts and even our godly desire to bless and build the people of God up are subject to what the Holy Spirit is saying. God moves through his Word; he did in the Creation and he still does now.

The best place to start is with what God is saying right now.

The Word of God
For me, a verse or selection of verses will emerge that will be my focus as I prepare. Usually the same verses will be the theme that I will lead with. I always try to

start fresh and allow the Holy Spirit to direct, either to lead me back to some recent teaching or to show me something new. He knows what he wants to say to his people; how to reveal Christ to them. (As I'm doing this, the preacher will doubtless be going through a similar process.)

As I spend time in this the Holy Spirit will suggest things and my thoughts will develop. Sometimes it is a slow process; sometimes a complete map of how the worship time should go will appear fully-formed. On a few occasions, I have received no particular guidance or possibly I've had to step in to lead at short notice, and then the Holy Spirit has moved 'in the moment'. It's beautiful when this happens because it emphasises that God is in control and that I'm not making it up.

It might be helpful to keep a notebook or diary to make notes of what God is saying – it can be very interesting to look back on. Try this:

Reflect on what teaching you are receiving at the moment and what God has been saying through your personal worship times. What scriptures are on your mind right now?

(Look at the scriptures you have and reflect on them prayerfully; read them in context. What do they mean? – What is God saying? Is this something specifically for you – or is it to share?

When you have a clear – or a fairly clear – idea of what the theme of the worship will be, you can start to look at songs and other elements and think about how the worship time might develop.)

It might seem obvious that the worship leader would need to communicate with the preacher or that the preacher would provide the Bible texts etc. Sometimes this happens and in some churches it's the norm, but it might not be appropriate.

In some congregations, the understanding of the Body of Christ is such that leading worship and preaching are regarded as different gifts or ministries, undertaken by different people, even though these will both be parts of the same 'act of worship'. They will each go in faith that the Holy Spirit will lead them individually and perfectly to a common point. He does – and it's amazing to see it happen, week after week. *There are diversities of gifts, says Paul, but the same Spirit* (1 Corinthians 12: 4).

Whatever the practice of a particular church, if you give the Holy Spirit space, he will bring the various gifts that different people have together to form a whole. There is no formula – no right way – to prepare for leading worship, except to say that it should be Biblically based. Our preparation for leading is part of our ongoing fellowship with our heavenly Father, and so is the worship in the congregation.

The temptation is to prepare 'half an hour of worship' or 'some songs', or even to rehearse a slick performance. But these miss the point of what worship is. As leaders we are only *enablers*, assisting God's people as they come together. It's far more important that we prepare ourselves than that we prepare material.

We might be looking for a *message* that God is giving to the people, but that's the preacher's role. In leading worship, our role is to open a conversation; to enable the people to hear and respond to what the Holy Spirit is saying.

Using the Bible

> *The word of God is living and powerful,*
> *and sharper than any two-edged sword, piercing*
> *even to the division of soul and spirit, and of*
> *joints and marrow, and is a discerner of the*
> *thoughts and intents of the heart.*

(Hebrews 4: 12)

The living Word of God is expressed in the Bible and it must be central to our worship together. In some congregations, the reading of the Holy Scriptures is very formal, in others less so; what matters is that the words are heard and understood and that in some way people are able to respond to them.

I try to choose songs that will supplement the Bible verses I'm using, so that a thought can be developed or examined. Since not everybody will have a Bible with them (and certainly not in the same version!), wherever possible I display the verses on screen so that everyone can read them. This is very helpful – and one of the ways in which modern technology can benefit worship.

There are other ways to make Bible reading fresh in worship and lots of books and materials available to explore. You might consider:

- Reading a passage together in unison – using the screen.
- Responsorial readings, where the leader reads a line and the people respond with the next line. Some Psalms are ideal for this.
- Dramatised readings can be good to bring certain passages and scenes to life.
- Shared readings where people read a verse each in turn can be good for smaller groups.
- Reading from different and unfamiliar translations

and various other creative responses to the Scriptures.

If these are used well, they can help people to engage with Scripture in fresh ways; where they are used poorly or in the wrong context, they can be quite disruptive and actually inhibit worship – so be careful with interactive techniques – often simply reading the verses is best.

> ...*man shall not live by bread alone; but man lives by every word that proceeds from the mouth of the LORD.*
>
> *(Deuteronomy 8: 3)*

The point is that we need to hear from God. When I'm leading, I'm very conscious that the Holy Spirit longs to engage with every person in the room, to bless them and to lead them forward in their Spiritual life.

Selecting Songs

> *Next to the Word of God, music deserves the highest praise. The gift of language combined with the gift of song was given to man that he should proclaim the Word of God through Music.*
>
> *(Martin Luther)*

The songs we sing are the expression of our worship together. We sing words that express our love to God, that declare our faith, that reveal Christ and that draw us into a close encounter with God. The tunes we sing and their musical arrangement both reflect our spiritual life in its cultural context and also help to form it.

That last sentence needs more explanation.

Music is very much an expression of culture. The kind of music we listen to in 2020 is different from what we would have listened to in 1920 or in 1820. Also, English expressions differ from Chinese, South Asian or Russian expressions, and even from American or Australian ones. The music we prefer will be different depending on our age, the part of the country we live in, our educational background and even our social class. We like to think that these things don't matter because we are *all one in Christ* but of course they do. If we are all going to participate in an expression of praise or intimacy with God, we have to do that in a way we all find comfortable and in a way we all understand and can share.

As we listen to particular types of music, this will affect our taste. In the same way, what we sing and how we sing it will affect other people – and some people, particularly some men, are uncomfortable about singing at all! We need to be sensitive to one another's needs; not everyone may be comfortable with everything we do, but it is important that we empower our brothers and sisters to worship God with music they can fully participate in.

We might not think that our personal taste has any place in worship. Perhaps in the New Jerusalem it won't, but here and now it does.

Why do we sing?

So, if taste is an important factor, is it okay for people not to sing at all if they feel uncomfortable?

We can't compel anyone, but singing is important in the Bible:

> *Make a joyful shout to the LORD, all you lands!*
> *² Serve the LORD with gladness; Come before His presence with singing.*
>
> *(Psalm 100: 1, 2)*

Singing is good for us. Recent research (Stacey & Brittain, 2002, Kreutz, 2003) shows that it makes us feel better by releasing endorphins; it can also increase lung capacity and reduce blood pressure and stress; it can even benefit the immune system. Singing together improves our social well-being – our sense of being part of a worshipping community; Stephen Clift, professor of

Health Education at Canterbury Christ Church University, writes:

> *"Just as walking is now prescribed, the benefits of singing for health are slowly being rediscovered by health practitioners."*

(Clift & Hancox, 2001)

So, singing is generally a good thing. In addition to being a healthy activity (which I'm sure we're relieved to hear), singing is good for us spiritually. When we sing praise to God we remind ourselves and each other of who he is and of his promises to us. Singing praise can change how we see our circumstances so that we can see them with Spiritual eyes. Also, as we discussed in detail in the previous chapter, declaring the praise of God is a powerful weapon against the powers of darkness. If some people feel embarrassed because they're not used to expressing themselves in that way, then it's important that we – together as a Body – try to move past these blockages.

There has been a big cultural shift in the last hundred years, and even in the last thirty, in the way worship songs are written and presented. Older hymns tend to use traditional English verse forms and regular (sometimes complex) rhyme schemes and metrical patterns. Often the pattern of the verses is quite repetitive, and sometimes there is a repeated chorus to bring us back to the central theme, but there is always an emphasis on the sense and meaning of the words. Sometimes this might seem over-elaborate to modern ears. Nowadays we prefer simple statements: sound-bites.

You are awesome in this place, mighty God.

Hymn tunes in the past were often a convenient way to deliver the words in a memorable form. Hymnists like Wesley, Newton and Cowper often set their hymns to the popular folk tunes of their day that people would easily pick up.

Many modern songs follow different patterns, a common one is:

verse - verse - chorus - bridge - chorus

This is a standard format for modern popular songs and feels very different from traditional hymns. Many people who are used to traditional styles can find modern patterns hard to follow. Sometimes the words can seem superficial or lacking clarity, and often the musical arrangements are more adapted for performance than for congregational singing. This is partly a generational effect: people who are used to listening to contemporary song styles find them easier to sing, while traditional hymns might seem long-winded and old fashioned.

It's worth commenting that some songs past and present aren't really fit for purpose; this is naturally more true of modern songs than older ones because time hasn't had so long to separate out the weak material that will eventually fall by the wayside. When we select songs, we need to make sure that they are suitable.

The problem with some older hymns is that language and culture have moved on. We're all probably guilty of singing things we don't understand, but when we're leading, we should avoid it. *In vain the first-born seraph tries/ To sound the depths of love divine.* It's a beautiful lyric, but how many people really know what it means?

We have to be sensitive when selecting songs to make them appropriate for the congregation as well as to the theme of the worship.

It's also worth re-stating that *worship is never about performance*. There are 'performance issues' to do with playing instruments in public and using amplification, etc., but these in themselves have nothing to do with worship. When we worship, God is our audience. We sing to him, and if no one else is in the congregation, it will make no difference.

My home congregation consists of many people who are mature in faith and years yet maintain an energetic and progressive outlook. When leading worship, I try to select songs that reflect this balance and are drawn from the rich store of worship material spanning three or four hundred years.

In selecting songs, my first priority is always that they develop thoughts that arise from the Scriptures. The words must express Biblical truth and not be misleading. I try to avoid songs that are either unclear or express sentiment rather than truth.

When Charles Wesley was writing hymns in the eighteenth century, his words often reflected the contents of his brother John's preaching – bearing in mind that many in his congregations were illiterate. Often the words of his hymns could stand as ministry in their own right. Few contemporary songs can match this depth of content.

It is important to select songs that reflect the differing needs of the congregation and that worshippers know the songs well or can learn them quickly, and that the words convey truth to those who are participating.

Testimony

> *We look not at the things which are seen, but at the things which are not seen: for the things which are seen are temporal [of the moment]; but the things which are not seen are eternal.*
>
> (2 Corinthians 4: 18 KJV, my parentheses)

Testimony is important because it is a personal statement of what God has done in a person's life. There are testimonies of salvation – what we might call someone's faith story – and there are day to day testimonies of how we experience and prove God in our lives. Both of these are an important part of worship. Think of Jonah's testimony (Chapter 5).

In an evangelistic event where the focus is on presenting the gospel of Jesus to an audience that includes many non-Christians, faith stories are especially valuable.

We can argue the evidence for the resurrection and people can take different positions on how they think the world was made, but in the end, we cannot prove the existence of God in a scientific sense. Science exists within particular boundaries – within the physical universe and the laws which define it. It can describe in detail what exists within that realm and how those things interact; it can describe mechanisms and processes through the use of logic and even work out the existence of things that haven't been discovered yet. These things are all good; but science can have nothing to say about spiritual things; *the things which are not seen*. Some scientists deny the existence of the spiritual realm because they can't access it with 'scientific' method. This is foolish.

Many people look to science to provide answers to questions for which it is not qualified. Science in itself can have nothing useful to say about the meaning of life or the existence of God, for example, though of course scientists may have opinions.

This is why testimony is so powerful. When people speak of God as a person who met them unexpectedly and transformed their lives, this cannot easily be contradicted or explained away. The truth that God cares for those who have no worth and gives them worth; that he meets those who are lost in depression and reveals their inner dignity and value is a truth that needs to be declared often and loudly.

I used to read the stories of people like David Wilkerson and Nicky Cruz, and sometimes be left feeling a bit 'unworthy'. My story seems mundane, by comparison. Not everyone can share an 'extreme testimony' but *I once was lost but now am found/ Was blind, but now I see* is something that we all share, even if our particular journey in Christ might be more evolutionary than revolutionary. The testimony in every case is Jesus: he makes the difference, just as the Word of God in the Bible points to Jesus.

When we meet together, we should share our ongoing story with one another. This encourages our brothers and sisters and builds the Body of Christ.

When I'm leading worship, I try to make time for brothers and sisters to share freely. It's very important when we come together that the whole body is able to minister to itself. Nobody should leave the meeting feeling that they haven't had an opportunity to share what the Holy Spirit has laid on their hearts. We'll discuss this in more detail in the next chapter.

Discussion 10

Suggest some effective ways to use the Bible in a worship time.

Share examples of how you have seen Scripture passages used effectively in worship.

Give an example of a time when you feel scripture wasn't used effectively.

How much do you think the worship leader should communicate with the preacher about what songs and other elements are used during the worship time?

What things should worship leaders consider when selecting songs?

Give an example of a time you heard personal testimony used well in a service.

11. Prayer

> *PRAYER: the Church's banquet, Angels' age,*
> *God's breath in man returning to his birth,*
> *The soul in paraphrase, heart in pilgrimage,*
> *The Christian plummet sounding heaven and earth;*
>
> *Engine against the Almighty, sinner's tower,*
> *Reversèd thunder, Christ-side-piercing spear,*
> *The six days' world transposing in an hour,*
> *A kind of tune which all things hear and fear;*
>
> *Softness, and peace, and joy, and love, and bliss,*
> *Exalted Manna, gladness of the best,*
> *Heaven in ordinary, man well-dressed,*
> *The milky way, the bird of Paradise,*
>
> *Church-bells beyond the stars heard, the soul's blood,*
> *The land of spices, something understood.*
>
> *George Herbert (1593-1633)*

George Herbert's meditation on prayer would take a lot of space to discuss in any detail; it's quite challenging and thought-provoking even though it's 400 years old. I'll start this chapter by looking at a few of the images he uses.

The Church's banquet. Banquets and feasts are themes that run through the Bible; sharing food with those we love is important. The Passover identified the families of God's people and enabled them to escape a curse (Exodus 12); God prepares a table for us in the presence of our enemies (Psalm 23: 5) and he brings us into his own banqueting house (Song of Solomon 4: 2). Jesus ate with his friends (John 12); with sinners (Mark 2) and with religious hypocrites (Luke 7: 36); he instituted a meal in his own memory (1 Corinthians 11: 23-26). At last, we are promised a wedding feast with the Lord Jesus himself, our Bridegroom (Revelation 1: 7). Prayer is our time of intimacy with God – our family time – when we can at the same time be completely open with him and enjoy the abundance of his blessing.

The Christian plummet sounding heaven and earth. A plummet is a depth gauge; a device for measuring the depth of water under a boat. In prayer, we can 'seek the face of God' and he can reveal his heart to us. For sounding we might say 'revealing' or 'exploring': through prayer we are able to discover the mind and character of God and deepen our knowledge of him.

Engine against the Almighty... That is, a siege engine or ram. The idea that we can 'lay siege' to God or bombard him with missiles is unusual – a strong image of prayer. But there are times when we need answers from God, and we don't get them. We should be shamelessly persistent in prayer according to Luke 11: 8 NLT.

Heaven in ordinary, man well-dressed. In other words, God has dressed himself in plain clothes ('ordinary') but we are covered in holy garments (see 2 Corinthians 5: 21). It is amazing that we can converse with God in our own words, in simple speech. We don't have to put on airs and graces. He has made us accepted in the beloved (Ephesians 1: 6).

Something understood. So often as we worship or read the Scriptures in a prayerful attitude, the Holy Spirit will drop something into our minds, perhaps new insight on something that we've been thinking about for a long time; perhaps something completely new. And there it is, fully-formed, a revelation: something understood.

Praying

> *At all times, pray by the power of the Spirit. Pray all kinds of prayers. Be watchful, so that you can pray. Always keep on praying for all of God's people.*
>
> *(Ephesians 6: 18 NIRV)*

What does Paul mean by all kinds of prayers?

Before we make a list, we need to start by looking briefly at what Jesus taught his disciples about prayer. The best-known and most concise teaching is the familiar passage in Matthew 6, the Lord's Prayer:

> *Our Father in heaven, hallowed be Your name. [10] Your kingdom come. Your will be done on earth as it is in heaven. [11] Give us this day our daily bread [12] and forgive us our debts, as we forgive our debtors. [13] And do not lead us into temptation, but deliver us from the evil one. For*

Yours is the kingdom and the power and the glory forever. Amen.

(Matthew 6: 9-13)

This is talking about personal prayer – he says, Go into your room … shut the door (v.6) – but the principles remain the same in other situations.

- *Our Father in heaven, hallowed be Your name.* Jesus' model prayer starts in the outer court with an acknowledgement that God is 'Our Father', followed by a statement of praise.

- *Your kingdom come.* Your will be done on earth as it is in heaven. We pray for God's work to be accomplished; for his reign to be established and for his purpose to be carried out.

- *Give us this day our daily bread.* We ask for provision.

- *Forgive us our debts, as we forgive our debtors.* We ask for forgiveness (not only for financial debts) and we also prepare ourselves to forgive others. This is to do with human relationships as much as about confessing sin to God.

- *And do not lead us into temptation, but deliver us from the evil one.* Of course, God doesn't 'lead us into temptation' – we do that by ourselves – but we acknowledge how easily we are side-tracked. We ask for spiritual protection from 'the evil one'.

- *For Yours is the kingdom and the power and the glory forever. Amen.* The final statement takes us back to where we started with an acknowledgement of God's power and authority in our lives and in the whole of creation.

In a few short statements, Jesus gives us a brief guide to prayer; to all kinds of prayer in fact; when we pray either on our own or when we lead others in prayer, it is useful to have this guide in mind. Although the words are familiar, it can still be helpful to have Matthew 6 open.

'All kinds of prayers'

I'm going to discuss a few different kinds of prayer that might be used in group worship. It is unlikely that they will all come in to every service, but we should be aware of different ways to approach our Father. I'll start by giving an overview of what each kind of prayer is like and how it is effective, then I'll give some suggestions for how they can be used in group worship.

Seeking the Father's face

> *Glory in His holy name; let the hearts of those rejoice who seek the LORD! Seek the LORD and His strength; seek His face evermore!*
>
> *(1 Chronicles 16: 10, 11 See also Psalm 105)*
>
> *If My people who are called by My name will humble themselves, and pray and seek My face,*

> *and turn from their wicked ways, then I will hear from heaven, and will forgive their sin and heal their land.*
>
> *(2 Chronicles 7: 14)*

Psalm 24: 6 declares that the 'children of Jacob' (in other words 'the people of God') are a nation who seeks God's face. Possibly David was being optimistic because we know that not all the people in the Old Testament did this; nevertheless, the thing that was supposed to make them different from other nations was that they *sought the face of God*. While this was only partly true of the ancient Israelites, it is very definitely true of the church.

We are Christians, members of – and living stones in – his holy temple, because we actively seek him. At some point, we have called out to him in the darkness and he has come to us. This is what makes us distinctive. We don't rely on a tradition or a religious identity; we actively seek him by faith when he isn't visible.

> *He who comes to God must believe that He is, and that He is a rewarder of those who diligently seek Him.*
>
> *He rewards those who diligently seek him. So the first stage of prayer is diligently to seek the face of God.*
>
> *(Hebrews 11: 6)*

2 Chronicles 7: 14 makes it clear that seeking God's face is part of an ongoing relationship, not a one-off

thing. Yahweh spoke to Solomon at the dedication of the Temple in Jerusalem and told him that when times are bad, *when I shut up heaven and there is no rain,* that the people must hum*ble themselves, pray, seek his face and turn from their sin.* This is one of the keys to spiritual revival. If we look back at the times God has moved in power in the UK; in South Wales and in the Hebrides, for example, these have started with small groups of people humbling themselves before God and seeking his face, often in private and sometimes over the course of many years.

Seeking the face of God is building a living relationship with him.

How do we do it?

Recently my home church has been urged by the Holy Spirit to seek God's face while facing some challenging situations. It has opened a new aspect of prayer for us.

We often like to come to prayer with our requests, our intercessions and our thanksgivings ready in a list. This is fine in itself, but these modes of prayer can become over-familiar – a sort of default setting. Our relationship with God can become static, so the Holy Spirit says: 'Seek my face.'

We didn't know what to make of this at first, so we sat in a room for an hour at a time, week after week and asked the Lord to show us what he wanted. And he did. Sometimes we sat more or less silently; sometimes scriptures would flow, or the Holy Spirit would give direction through Spiritual gifts. We kept a record of these things and built up a clear picture of God's mind in that particular matter. It took time but it was exciting and added a powerful new dimension to our life as a church.

I'm sure that it isn't strictly necessary to sit in silence and wait for 'inspiration' – that's just how we did it – but it is necessary to come to the Father without any agenda or preconceived ideas, and that is the hard thing. We found the key aspects to be *diligence*, *humility* and *honesty*. *Patience* is also important.

Seeking God's face in this way as a group leads to building up the Body of Christ and deepening our relationships with the Lord and with each other.

'Waiting on the Lord'

> *Wait on the LORD; be of good courage, and He shall strengthen your heart; wait, I say, on the LORD!*
>
> *(Psalm 27: 14)*
>
> *Those who wait on the LORD shall renew their strength; they shall mount up with wings like eagles, they shall run and not be weary, they shall walk and not faint.*
>
> *(Isaiah 40: 31)*

'Some of the early Pentecostals would have 'tarrying' meetings. They would sit and wait for the Holy Spirit to fall on them as he did on the disciples in Acts 2; sometimes they would wait for hours for the Holy Spirit to 'fall' and bless them. While I'm sure this was an act of faith and it doubtless led to a blessing, it shows a misunderstanding of Scripture and the gifts of the Holy Spirit. We don't have to sit in a room and wait for God to do something he has already done.

The phrase 'wait on the Lord' can give an image similar to this, of people waiting in expectancy for something to happen, waiting for the arrival of some blessing or a sign. 'I need to make a decision' we might say, 'so I'm waiting on the Lord for guidance.' God promises to guide us, but not by our passively 'waiting' for him. (Incidentally, he doesn't promise us *guidance* as we wait on him, but *strength*.)

We wait on the Lord as a waiter waits at table; we wait as servants for instructions; we deliberately place ourselves at his disposal. In this sense, waiting is an active, not a passive thing. We are waiting with the expectation that God will do something through us, not to us. This is why he promises us strength: as we make ourselves available to God without reservation, we are likely to find ourselves in uncomfortable situations. He takes us out of our comfort-zone so that he can test our faith and our reliance on him.

> *I have learned in whatever state I am, to be content:* [12] *I know how to be abased, and I know how to abound. Everywhere and in all things I have learned both to be full and to be hungry, both to abound and to suffer need.* [13] *I can do all things through Christ who strengthens me.*
>
> *(Philippians 4: 11-13)*

I can do all things… Paul isn't saying that Christ turns him into some kind of superhero: he won't make us 'Ministry Man' or 'Worship Woman'. But he wants us to be assured that whatever God requires of us, he will resource. He is our provider. Notice that Paul has learned how to be *abased* as well as to *abound* and how to be *hungry* as well as *full*; the length, breadth and height of our experience with God contains many different gifts and many different kinds of provision.

How do we 'wait on God'?

> *Your ears shall hear a word behind you, saying, "This is the way, walk in it," Whenever you turn to the right hand or whenever you turn to the left.*
>
> (Isaiah 30: 21)

A person who has a servant has no difficulty in making his needs known with a word of command, the snap of a finger or perhaps with more detailed instructions. In the same way, God makes his instructions to us clear; they only become obscure when we don't listen.

The first thing is to know what he has told us to do in the Bible. Jesus' commands to his disciples are few but far-reaching: love God, love one another; make disciples; preach the gospel; heal the sick; keep the Communion. These are our 'standing orders'; they aren't going to change.

The next thing is to know what he's telling me to do today. These will never contradict the standing orders but will supplement them in some way. We need to make ourselves available for God to speak to us in an attitude of expectant listening. Just as a workplace might have a staff briefing at the beginning of the day, we can do the same. First thing in the morning, have a briefing with Father and ask him what he wants from you today. This is waiting with purpose.

Thanksgiving

> *Rejoice always, [17] pray without ceasing, [18] in everything give thanks; for this is the will of God in Christ Jesus for you.*
>
> *(1 Thessalonians 5: 16-18)*
>
> *Tell God what you need and thank him for all he has done.*
>
> *(Philippians 4: 6b NLT)*

In everything give thanks. Coming as it does in one of Paul's lists it's easy to dismiss this as a rhetorical flourish, almost a throw-away line. But there are no throw-away lines in Paul's teaching. Thanksgiving is key to our prayer life and central to our identity as Christians. We must constantly remind ourselves and each-other that God is our provider: he provides for us abundantly and he does it in grace. There is no sense that we deserve his blessing, but he gives it to us anyway.

If we find ourselves, as sometimes we do, in difficult circumstances – illness, bereavement, or something else that we have no control over – we are experiencing what it means to be human. But these hardships, though they might be devastating to us, fade into insignificance by comparison with what God has done for us in Jesus Christ. He has given us everlasting love, confidence in salvation and the hope of glory, and these are not the common experience of humankind.

This is why Paul says in the verse quoted above from Philippians 4 (in the New King James version):

> *Be anxious for nothing, but in everything by prayer and supplication, with thanksgiving, let your requests be made known to God; and the peace of God, which surpasses all understanding, will guard your hearts and minds through Christ Jesus.*
>
> *(Philippians 4: 6, 7)*

By prayer and supplication (that is, by all kinds of prayer) with thanksgiving, let your requests be made known to God. Our requests are made in an envelope of thanksgiving.

These verses start with *Be anxious for nothing* and go on to speak of *the peace of God that passes understanding*. They come as a package. Anxiety is the default mode of the human race, it is natural for us, but when we cultivate the awareness of God's provision and encourage it in each other we can build a culture of thanksgiving. This influences the quality of our worship and our testimony of Christ.

How to do it
There's an old-fashioned hymn which sounds annoyingly trite to modern listeners:

> *Count your blessings, name them one by one*
> *And it will surprise you what the Lord has done.*

"What have I got to be thankful for?" As the song suggests, you can actually make a list, starting with the basic things (food, shelter, sleep, etc.) and working your way up.

It may be that even those basic things are lacking; maybe you or someone you love is very sick; perhaps you are short of food. These emergencies can overwhelm and preoccupy; they can make prayer difficult. The real extremities of life test what we believe – what we have – and the most important things we have, our identity and our faith in God, cannot be changed by our circumstances.

I can hold on to this: God is my Father and he loves me. Let us prove his faithfulness by trusting him for life's necessities.

Intercession
Intercession is praying for other people; more accurately, it's representing them before God. If we were to stand before a judge on a criminal charge, a barrister would represent us – he or she would speak on our behalf, in our defence. This is intercession – to stand between someone and their judge.

There are several examples in the Bible of people interceding. In Numbers 16, when Korah and his followers rebelled against Moses, Yahweh instructed Moses and Aaron to get out of the way so that he could destroy them (vv. 20, 21), but they refused;

> *Then they fell on their faces, and said, "O God, the God of the spirits of all flesh, shall one man sin, and You be angry with all the congregation?"*
>
> *(Numbers 16: 22)*

It took a lot of courage to stand in front of God and effectively challenge him in that way; it also took faith in God's compassion for his people. We might read this as God testing Moses' and Aaron's faith, but however we understand it, they stood between the wrath of God and the people. This is what intercessors do.

It is what Jesus did for us on the Cross:

> *For Christ also suffered once for sins, the just for the unjust, that He might bring us to God....*
>
> *(1 Peter 3: 18a)*

He stood in the way of God's righteous anger and took it upon himself so that it would not fall on us.

Paul declares that he would be willing to lose his own salvation if it meant that his fellow Jews might be saved:

> *For I could wish that I myself were accursed from Christ for my brethren, my countrymen according to the flesh ...*
>
> *(Romans 9: 3)*

The heart of an intercessor is willing to change places with the person he or she is praying for. This is the compassion that Christ has, and this is what makes intercession powerful. Jesus said that we should love one another in the way that he loves us (John 13: 34) – when we do this we release the power of God.

As we intercede for others, the Holy Spirit intercedes for us:

> *The Spirit ... helps in our weaknesses. For we do not know what we should pray for as we ought, but the Spirit Himself makes intercession for us with groanings which cannot be uttered ... He makes intercession for the saints according to the will of God.*
>
> (Romans 8: 26, 27)

We pray to God out of our limited human perception. We don't see with God's eyes, and mostly we don't understand what the truth of the matter is. Whether we speak fine words; whether we pray 'in tongues' or whether we just grunt meaninglessly makes little difference; the most beautifully composed or the longest-winded prayers are all equal nonsense in themselves. The Holy Spirit knows what we mean at the deepest level; he knows our heart-cry and renders that to the Father.

In John 14, 15 and 16 the Holy Spirit is referred to as an *Advocate* or *Counsellor* (John 14: 15, 16 and 26; John 15: 26, and John 16: 7 – *Comforter* in the KJV; different translations use different words):

> *Very truly I tell you, it is for your good that I am going away. Unless I go away, the Advocate will not come to you; but if I go, I will send him to you.*
>
> *(John 16: 7 NIV)*

We pray to God and the Holy Spirit takes our thoughts and words and presents them to our Father. When we are made aware of somebody's need, we feel the 'burden' of that situation and bring it before the Father in prayer. We act in love and grace and at the prompting of the Holy Spirit and he takes our prayers and represents them to God. From first to last, God inspires the process: our desire to pray for someone; the words we speak, and the 'message' that the Father receives. We can be sure that if the Holy Spirit inspires us to pray, that prayer will be effective, and if we are willing to go where they are – to stand in the gap – we will unleash the power of heaven.

Supplication

Supplication is praying for our needs. Supplication goes with thanksgiving – see above (Philippians 4: 6, 7).

We all have material needs. We need clothing, housing, food; we probably need transport and some other things. God has promised to provide for all our needs. Jesus says:

> *Ask, and it will be given to you; seek, and you will find; knock, and it will be opened to you. For*

*everyone who asks receives, and he who seeks
finds, and to him who knocks it will be opened.*

(Matthew 7: 7)

*Whatever things you ask in prayer, believing,
you will receive.*

(Matthew 21: 22)

Do we need to ask for things that God has already promised to give us?

This is a fair question, because the Bible is quite clear that God will provide what we need as we serve him and also that he will meet our material needs; these promises are repeated time and time again in Scripture. God is our Father; he loves us; of course, he will provide for us. It is a matter of faith and of applying the Bible's promises to our lives.

Nevertheless, Jesus tells us quite clearly to ask:

*If you abide in Me, and My words abide in you,
you will ask what you desire, and it shall be done
for you.*

(John 15: 7)

Many people say that prayer of this kind is more effective when it is detailed and specific. Our Father will not withhold his blessing from us, but he loves it when we spend the time to talk about our needs with him. This deepens our fellowship.

We must ask God for our specific needs in faith, trusting in his promise to *supply all [our] need according to*

His riches in glory (Philippians 4: 19). In the end, this kind of prayer changes us, not God – because he has promised to act anyway. It's great to tell Father about our needs and worries, and then see him intervene to meet them.

Prayer of this kind brings us back to reliance on his Word and the promises he has made; we can be explicit in our prayer in that we are asking 'according to his word' and even give thanks in advance for the answer.

Prayer in Worship

When we're leading worship, we should include opportunities for people to pray, but what form this will take will depend on who is there and the type of meeting. Here are a few pointers:

Before the service.
It's good for the worship leader or team to pray in the room before the service. We know that God will be present according to his promise in Matthew 18: 20 that *where two or three are gathered together in My name, I am there in the midst of them*, so we're not 'asking God to be there' or anything like that, however it can help us focus and to be aware of the needs of the people who will be present. If we begin a worship session in an attitude of intercession and expectation, we will be more effective as leaders in worship.

At the beginning of the service.
We should acknowledge the Lord's presence as we open the service. It's normal to ask his blessing on the

gathering, possibly linked with a suitable scripture reading. I like to pray that God will take control of every aspect of the meeting – every word, thought and action – and that he will draw from us worship that is acceptable to him. Remember the image from Song of Solomon 4, of the wind blowing into the closed garden so that the fragrance would flow out.

During the service.

There should be time to pray together. This can be done in several different ways and might contain liturgical elements. In my home church, our prayer times often include the following:

Open prayer[12]. We wait quietly as members of the congregation lead prayer as they feel the directing of the Spirit.

Directed Prayer. Sometimes we will direct open prayer either by displaying headings to pray for – these might be current concerns in the congregation, matters of local or national concern, or items in the news – or by asking individuals to lead prayer for particular things.

Liturgical elements. Sometimes the worship leader will insert a set prayer such as a collect as a way of drawing prayerful thoughts together. It's also common to close a meeting with a blessing or benediction, or with the Grace.

Group Prayer. Sometimes we will divide the congregation into groups of three or four and ask them to pray or seek the Lord's face for a short time. This may be followed by a feedback session where groups can share any pictures or other Gifts that may have been given. We would normally use this in a special prayer meeting rather than in regular worship.

Small groups can also be a way to do 'open prayer' in larger congregations.

Prayer Board, etc. Sometimes people are asked to write prayers on slips of paper and then stick them on a board or put them in a pile, box, etc. This might be used for intercessions or for confession of sin. (In the case of confessions, the papers are folded so that they can't be read, and then destroyed to demonstrate God's forgiveness.)

Incidental Prayers. We will sometimes pray for the speaker as he gets up, especially if he or she is visiting. Sometimes people will ask for prayer or for permission to pray for someone else. We should be open and flexible.

Following 2 Timothy 5: 22, we should not lay hands on anybody without their permission; this can be difficult for people if they don't know what to expect or if they are not comfortable with physical contact.

At the end of the service.
Some messages end with a direct call to respond – possibly they all should – *Today, if you hear my voice....* Prayer (and music) at the end of the service should reflect this. Sometimes it might be necessary to have a 'prayer line' where people need to express their response to God's word by stepping forward and receiving prayer – perhaps for commissioning or a blessing.

The 'Altar Call'. (There isn't actually an altar, of course.) This is where people step forward after hearing the word to give their lives to Christ either for the first time or in a rededication. In this case they might receive prayer, but the important thing is that they pray, so that someone else can hear them, inviting Jesus Christ into their lives. It's possible for there to be more than one opportunity for people to respond during the course of a meeting.

Prayer is a basic part of worship. It is us, as members of the congregation, approaching God in our own words; it's what makes worship a conversation. How it is handled varies greatly depending on the type of service, the context and the character of the worship leader, but it is necessary to make substantial time available for prayer in some form.

Discussion 11

Is there anything in Herbert's poem that speaks to you about 'prayer'?

- Can you find another poem or artwork about prayer that you find helpful?

Is it possible to be a member of the church without being a believer?

Thanksgiving to God should be the context of much of our lives. He is our Provider, our 'Good, good Father'.

- How can we express thanks to God in congregational worship?

Philippians 4: 4-13 is an important passage about prayer and thanksgiving. How can this be used in worship?

Many worship services invite or require corporate prayer – opportunities for the whole church to pray together.

- How can you incorporate prayer into a worship service?

12. Spiritual Gifts

The Holy Spirit bestows gifts for service to men.
Christ gives the gifted men to the churches.

(Scofield, 1909)

The subject of Spiritual gifts is still oddly controversial in some circles of the church, yet the teaching of the Bible is clear. This chapter is an overview of Paul's teaching on Spiritual gifts and the Body of Christ in 1 Corinthians chapters 12 to 14.

Now concerning spiritual gifts, brethren, I do not want you to be ignorant.

(1 Corinthians 12: 1)

1 Corinthians 12, 13 and 14, along with Romans 12 and Ephesians 4 explain in detail what the Gifts of the Holy Spirit are and how they should be used.

When leading a congregation in worship, we must be aware of what the Holy Spirit is doing and saying. He has been with us before the event and during the time we spent preparing and he's with us – in us and around us – as we lead. He's aware of our circumstances, and of how the rest of the congregation is doing; he has been with each of them too, preparing them for what he has to say. He will bring something through the interaction of worship to meet all our needs. And if we allow him, he'll use us to do it. That's a privilege.

Somebody described the action of the Holy Spirit in a congregation as hovering like a bird above the people and directing his gifts to where they are needed. As one person has a need, he will lead another to meet it; one person may be given a word in tongues and another will be given the interpretation for the benefit of a third person. God is among his people to nurture and to teach, to direct and to heal, in older translations the word is *edify* – and he does this through the people themselves. In this activity, the person at the front is not so much a leader as a convener.

Every congregation needs leaders – but there is no hierarchy in Christ. He is the head; we are his body. No one is above anyone else, though people have different roles. In the congregation, the Body of Christ serves the Body of Christ. We minister one to another.

When we're leading worship, we need to understand this. Our role is to enable that free movement of the Holy Spirit.

The Work of the Holy Spirit in the Body of Christ (1 Corinthians 12)

Two Greek words are used interchangeably in 1 Corinthians 12: *pneumatika* (v.1), meaning 'spiritual qualities' and *kharismata* (v.4), meaning 'qualities of grace and beauty'. We interpret both to mean 'gifts of the Holy Spirit'.

The Holy Spirit is the presence and essence of God himself, yet sometimes we almost dismiss him as 'the Third Person in the Trinity', as if he only managed a bronze medal, or we think of him impersonally as *power*. Yet he is the power that created everything that exists, and he has made us his *tabernacle*; his *temple*; his holy place. It's not surprising that his presence is shown in supernatural happenings: if God is living in you, you are much more than you were before.

The gifts he gives us also demonstrate his character; they are full of grace – generosity and kindness – and also beauty. Everything the Holy Spirit does is beautiful: *he is altogether lovely.*

The middle section of Chapter 12 (vv. 12-27) shows how the Holy Spirit brings believers together to form the Body of Christ, which behaves a bit like a natural, physical body. Each part – each organ, limb or faculty – has a different use and is dependent on all the others. Think of the Holy Spirit as being like the blood supply to the body.

> *There are diversities of gifts, but the same Spirit.* [5] *There are differences of ministries, but the same Lord.* [6] *And there are diversities of activities, but it is the same God who works all in all.* [7] *But the manifestation of the Spirit is given to each one for the profit of all.*

(1 Corinthians 12: 4-7)

As members of Christ's Body, we are all given gifts; these gifts distinguish us from one another in the same way that an eye is distinguished from a foot. Everybody is given a gift – an ability to serve – (1 Corinthians 12: 7, 11, 27) freely by the Holy Spirit as he sees fit. And as an eye does not resemble a foot, different spiritual gifts look and feel very different from one another.

Spiritual gifts are not the same as natural talents (nobody ever had a 'talent' for prophecy) and they are not chosen by the people they are given to. 'Ministry' in the church is simply the use of whatever gift each person has received (see Romans 12: 4-8) for the common benefit.

The gifts we are given suit our personality. If someone has the gift to be an evangelist, it's likely that they were good at communicating before they came to Christ. But the Holy Spirit also works to change us, sometimes very deeply. It's not unusual for someone with a violent and aggressive past to be given a gentle and nurturing gift. When this happens, we know God is at work.

Spiritual Gifts are by definition full of grace and beauty; they are also spiritual, just as the Body of Christ is spiritual.

> *For to one is given the word of wisdom through the Spirit, to another the word of knowledge through the same Spirit, [9] to another faith by the same Spirit, to another gifts of healings by the same Spirit, [10] to another the working of miracles, to another prophecy, to another discerning of spirits, to another different kinds of tongues, to another the interpretation of tongues. [11] But one and the same Spirit works all these things, distributing to each one individually as He wills.*
>
> *(1 Corinthians 12: 8-11)*

Of the nine gifts listed here (and the list isn't complete – other gifts are mentioned elsewhere) six – *word of wisdom, word of knowledge, prophecy, discerning spirits, tongues* and *interpretation of tongues* – are to do with communication; while the other three – *faith, healing* and *miracles* – are mostly to do with action. Many of these gifts are demonstrated in the Acts of the Apostles.[13]

When the church is functioning healthily, these gifts will be active – they are normal among Christians. It is common in the Book of Acts and quite common even today for someone newly saved or baptised to prophesy or speak in tongues, often with no knowledge of what they are doing. We should expect this.

Word of Wisdom is typically a word or message given that unlocks a door to ministry or provision. A good example is the Apostle Paul and the 'Man from Macedonia' in Acts 16: 9-10. Paul saw a vision which revealed to him the need to go across to Macedonia; his obedience to this led ultimately to the salvation of the Philippian Jailer. Other examples might be in Acts 8: 26 to Philip and in Acts 9: 10-15 to Ananias concerning Paul's conversion.

"***Word of Knowledge***," as Donna Kazenske writes[14], "is the God-given ability to receive from God … the facts concerning something that is humanly impossible for us to know anything about. It's a gift of the "word" of knowledge. It is not the gift of knowledge."

The last sentence in this quotation is important. God will often put a piece of information into a person's mind concerning someone else. When this is shared, it will have a profound effect on the person who receives it while meaning almost nothing to the person sharing it. This gift is very common in prayer times: often, as we pray for one another, the Lord will give us a form of words or an image with special significance to another person in the room.

Faith. Different kinds of faith are described in the Bible. We can't come to Christ and be saved without faith (Ephesians 2: 8), nor can we please God. In 1 Corinthians 12 Paul is writing about the kind of faith also mentioned in Hebrews 11 and that Jesus said could move mountains. This faith is the *substance of things hoped for, the evidence of things unseen* (Hebrews 11: 1 KJV). In other words, it takes dreams and aspirations, things that are hypothetical or hoped for, and turns them into concrete *reality ... so that things which are seen were not made of things which do appear* (Hebrews 11: 3 KJV).

There are many accounts of this in Scripture (for example Elijah on Mt Carmel – 1 Kings 18: 33-35). Any work for God, from sharing Christ with a friend to building a new congregation of a thousand people, starts with a vision which must be followed in faith.

The righteous live by faith (Romans 1: 17). We should seek to prove God – our dependence on Him and His provision – every day. The gift of faith is the ability to claim from God what seems to be impossible and to make it happen.

Healing. Healing is part of the character of God and is revealed in Exodus 15: 16 as one of God's compound names: *Yahweh-Rophe* – I AM your Healer.

Jesus demonstrates this by pouring out compassion and healing upon the people he meets; the Holy Spirit gives the same gift to us. Sometimes it is mediated through prayer (James 5: 15-16), sometimes through a word of faith or with an action of devotion or obedience to God, but as in the Gospels, God will rarely work in the same way more than once. He doesn't want us to rely on formulae but to trust Him.

It's worth noting that often these gifts work together. Healing often goes alongside *Faith* and a *Word of Knowledge*.

Miracles – literally *works of power*. Again, there is an obvious overlap with other spiritual gifts: when Peter and John healed the lame man at the temple gate, it's safe to say it was a miracle. A good example of a 'non-medical' miracle was Elijah and the widow's oil (1 Kings 17: 13-16).

Many Christians today can describe instances where God has intervened miraculously. A friend of mine – a former pastor – was able to drive his family home in poor weather, in a car that later turned out to have had disconnected points and shouldn't have run at all. At the time, he couldn't understand why it wouldn't do more than 40 miles per hour. There are many such stories; small incidents that are deeply significant at the time.

Miracles cannot be explained in natural terms.

Prophecy. A prophecy is a *Spiritual utterance.* In the Bible, this generally means two things: it can be *foretelling* future events, such as in Isaiah 7: 14 (*Behold, the virgin shall conceive and bear a Son, and shall call His name Immanuel*); it can also be the *forth-telling* of the mind of God such as when Jesus confronted the religious rulers' hypocrisy in Matthew 9: 4. Prophecies that come in a worship service, however, are nearly always *forth-telling*. In this sense, the prophecy should rarely come as a complete surprise but will confirm what God is saying in other ways.

All of the 'communicating' gifts are in some sense prophetic; they are ways in which God speaks to us; they are keys to our life as the Body of Christ. When we meet to worship, we need to hear from the Holy Spirit in each other; in this way we worship in *Spirit and in truth.* When we speak it should be the *utterances of God* (1 Peter 4: 11).

If we allow the Holy Spirit to empower us and inform our words and actions, much of what we do ought to be prophetic because it reveals aspects of the character of God.

Discerning Spirits. Sometimes people say things that are just obviously *wrong.* These we can dismiss, but sometimes people say things that don't directly contradict the Bible but are still wrong. We can learn how to identify some of these, but we always need to rely on the witness of the Holy Spirit to tell us whether a word is from God or not – we can never completely rely on our ability to 'figure it out'. The things of the Spirit must be *spiritually discerned* (1 Corinthians 2: 14).

This is an important gift for worship leaders because it is essential to know when to encourage someone to contribute, when to linger on a thought or when to move the worship on.

Tongues. There are three different Spiritual gifts that might be called 'the gifts of tongues'. In Acts 2, Peter and the disciples went out onto the streets of Jerusalem, filled with the Holy Spirit and spoke in *other tongues*; they were bringing God's word to the people who miraculously heard it in their own languages (Acts 2: 5, 6). This is a very specific gift to bring unbelievers to salvation, it is sometimes, though rarely, seen today.

When we meet Jesus personally and he fills us with the Holy Spirit, he may give us a private prayer language with which we can speak intimately with God; this is probably what Paul means in 1 Corinthians 14: 18. But the main teaching in Chapters 13 and 14 is the *prophetic utterance of tongues* in the context of the church assembly. This use of tongues is different from private prayer in that it is clearly intended to be interpreted to others. When we meet together everything should build up the Body of Christ. If we pray, we should do it so that others can hear; when we speak in tongues it should not be a private thing but for *interpretation* so that everyone can share in it.

It's possible also to *sing in tongues* (1 Corinthians 14: 15) as we lift our hearts to the Lord in worship.

Interpretation. When such a prophetic tongue is given, someone should always be present to interpret it;

sometimes the speaker will interpret his or her own tongue, though this is unusual. The interpretation will take the form of a prophetic word that builds up the church in some way, and as with prophecy, the Holy Spirit usually speaks to confirm what he is saying elsewhere. In practice, it is not unusual for the gift of *interpretation* to be given to a person before tongues itself.

Note that the interpretation of a message in tongues is not a 'translation'.

With each of these spiritual gifts there are those who have a particular gifting or ministry. Someone might often pray words of knowledge; another might be used often in healing, another might be able to sing prophetically. But God divides to each as he chooses, and he may give gifts to different people.

As we read these chapters in Corinthians, we find that God has given and will continue to give whatever gifts are needed at the time they are required for us to be edified – encouraged, strengthened, taught and corrected in Christ and to enable us to move forward in evangelism and righteous works.

With Love (1 Corinthians 13)

As we read the Bible we should try, as far as we can, to understand its original context in order to understand why the writers use the words they do. The church's experience in Corinth would have been different from their experience in Ephesus for example, and both would have been very different from our experience today. So, we ought to find out what we can about who the Corinthians were and what their world was like. Of course, it is impossible to do this perfectly; we can never step out of our 21st Century skins and assume 1st Century Corinthian identities. But if we could, what would it have been like?

Biblical Corinth was a busy port city on the *isthmus* (the narrow strip of land) that joins mainland Greece with the Peloponnese; it had two harbours one facing west and the other east. The original Greek city had been destroyed in 146 BC and the city Paul wrote to and visited was a Roman colony, though it was at the very heart of the Greek world about fifty miles from Athens. Most of the people would have been culturally Greek but there would have been a large number of Romans, as well as traders from all over the Mediterranean. There was an established community of Jewish traders which had recently been increased by Jews expelled from Rome by the Emperor Claudius in AD49 (six years before this letter) among whom were Aquila and Priscilla, Paul's friends. Corinth was an important city strategically, economically and culturally. Major land and sea battles had been fought nearby and the Isthmian Games were held every two years.

A famous temple to Aphrodite, the Greek goddess of Love had once stood on top of the *Acrocorinth*, the rocky hill that dominated the city, but in Paul's time it was ruined and only a small temple remained. It had been reported, by Strabo, an ancient travel writer, that there were a thousand prostitutes in the temple. (These would have been given to the goddess as gifts by rich citizens or visitors and would have served as sex-slaves. The money they made would have gone into the temple treasury.) This may have been true once, but it certainly wasn't in Paul's time; the temple was far too small.

Nevertheless, there was still a cult of Aphrodite, and with many visitors to the city from all over the world, doubtless there were still plenty of women and men for hire above the city's many taverns and wine shops. Corinth was a large and cosmopolitan city; it had a reputation for its relaxed 'anything goes' attitude to morality.

There was a large and active temple to Poseidon where the Isthmian Games were held, and other temples included those to Apollo, Hermes and Isis. There was also an ancient sanctuary of Demeter, the 'earth goddess', home to one of the ancient 'mystery' cults. The famous Oracle of Delphi was a hundred miles or so to the north-west and may have been influential.

All this gives a sense of the city behind Paul's letters; Corinth would have been an exciting and possibly dangerous place, a challenging environment for the early Christian church.

> *Though I speak with the tongues of men and of angels, but have not love, I have become a sounding brass or a clanging cymbal.* [2] *And though I have the gift of prophecy, and understand all mysteries and all knowledge, and though I have all faith, so that I could remove mountains, but have not love, I am nothing.*

> *³ And though I bestow all my goods to feed the poor, and though I give my body to be burned, but have not love, it profits me nothing.*
>
> *(1 Corinthians 13: 1-3)*

Speaking with the *tongues of men and angels* was probably not as unusual for the Corinthians as it is for us. There would have been religious ceremonies associated with Delphi or with the cult of Demeter where people would be moved to states of altered consciousness. Some of these would have been induced by drugs or alcohol, some would have involved group hysteria; all were demonic in one way or another.

In the same way *prophecy* would have been familiar, as would *speaking mysteries* and *words of knowledge*. The Delphic Oracle was notoriously ambiguous when it came to these things (in fact a 'Delphic utterance' has come to mean a kind of riddle). Much Greek and Roman religion was to do with cultural tradition or group or family identity rather than actual spiritual power, but occult practices and quests for hidden knowledge were always present and seductive – then as now.

But Christ offered more than this.

All of these things are meaningless without *love*, Paul says; then he goes on to define what he means by *love*, and it isn't Aphrodite. Paul uses the Greek word *agapē*, which usually meant a strong social or family bond, and gives it a new meaning for the church.[15]

Jesus explains this in John 15: 12 - *love one another as I have loved you*; he gave his life willingly to save us. In

Chapter 13 Paul breaks love down for us. To the Corinthians in AD55 this would have been a radical teaching, and it still is to us: the kind of love only found in the Body of Christ, because it depends on Jesus' sacrifice.

> *Love suffers long and is kind; love does not envy; love does not parade itself, is not puffed up; ⁵ does not behave rudely, does not seek its own, is not provoked, thinks no evil; ⁶ does not rejoice in iniquity, but rejoices in the truth; ⁷ bears all things, believes all things, hopes all things, endures all things.*

(1 Corinthians 13: 4-7)

For the Corinthian Christians and also for us there is to be patience and kindness always; no envying of other people's gifts or talents; no pride or grandstanding – this can be tough for worship leaders, when everyone's looking at you and telling you that you're talented. *Love does not seek its own* – it doesn't have to force its way. If you have a Spiritual gift to share, God will make space and people will hear it in the right place.

Love is not easily provoked. Don't get angry or feel slighted if someone steals your time-slot or makes a comment about you; love thinks no evil. Check your thoughts: what are you thinking about right now? (Remember Philippians 4: 8: *whatever things are true, whatever things are noble, whatever things are just, whatever things are pure, whatever things are lovely, whatever things are of good report, if there is any virtue and if there is anything praiseworthy — meditate on these things.)*

Love does not rejoice in iniquity but rejoices in the truth; the Word of God given by the Holy Spirit is always truth. He will never contradict himself or cause hurt. When we come into the presence of God, into his holy place, he will only speak to us in words that build and edify in the holy place of worship; never to condemn or judge.

Paul continues describing love in more general ways; how it affects our lives outside of church meetings; *love bears all things*. We might have a difficult boss or an overbearing pastor, but the Corinthians kept many slaves – and some members of the church were slaves themselves; love bears all things: imagine saying that in a place where you could be bought or sold.

Love believes all things. Well, it rejoices in truth: it isn't gullible. We are defined by our faith, by what we believe, not by what we don't believe. Some Christians tell us at length what they don't believe, but it's far better to celebrate what we do believe. We believe in the saving love and grace of our Lord Jesus Christ and therefore we must believe in one another. Even when someone accuses a brother or sister – and even if the accusation turns out to be true! – We must believe in them, even if they mess up repeatedly. Why? *Because Jesus does*. There are situations where this is especially important. If we find ourselves persecuted and subject to all kinds of accusations, we must stand by one another. Where a brother or sister is recovering from a serious setback –

perhaps they're coming out of prison or fighting an addiction – we must believe in them. This isn't to believe the rubbish that people sometimes say when they are frightened, frustrated or fallen, but to believe that the Spirit of God in them is bigger than their tendency to fail. This is the love of Christ that Paul describes, and it's hard work.

Love hopes all things. We know that *Hope does not disappoint because the love of God is poured out in our hearts* (Romans 5: 11). Christians are identified by their hope; hope for ourselves: Christ, our *hope of glory* (Colossians 1: 27), and also for one another. *We rejoice in hope* (Romans 12: 12). This hope is not a kind of hoping for the best 'I hope they play our song' kind of hope. It's an investment in the future, a kind of spiritual pension fund that won't be eaten up by unscrupulous money-dealers.

> *I know the thoughts that I think toward you,*
> *says the LORD, thoughts of peace and not of evil,*
> *to give you a future and a hope.*
>
> (Jeremiah 29: 11)

Hope is one of the most important aspects of the gospel in a world that often seems formless, void and wrapped in darkness.

Love endures all things. The early Christians at Corinth had a lot on their plates. The Romans distrusted them; the Jews hated them; the Greeks thought they were mad and a disruptive influence. Relatively speaking, we have an easy time of it here in the West (not so much elsewhere). Paul says:

> *Yet indeed I also count all things loss for the excellence of the knowledge of Christ Jesus my Lord, for whom I have suffered the loss of all things, and count them as rubbish, that I may gain Christ.*
>
> *(Philippians 3: 8)*

That is the context of our worship in the Body of Christ, in the fulness of his love and the freedom of the Holy Spirit. We think about Christians under persecution and wonder at their rock-solid faith; at the price they pay simply for being themselves. Yet the truth is that 'to be born again, first you have to die'; unless we have suffered the loss of all things, we haven't put on Christ.

> *Love never fails. But whether there are prophecies, they will fail; whether there are tongues, they will cease; whether there is knowledge, it will vanish away. [9] For we know in part and we prophesy in part. [10] But when that which is perfect has come, then that which is in part will be done away.*
>
> *(1 Corinthians 13: 8-10)*

Love never fails (v.8) – but spiritual gifts will. The demonic ones without love are just a noise anyway, but even the Holy Spirit-given gifts will fail. Prophecies will be fulfilled; all our misunderstandings will be resolved, and the wisest sayings will seem obvious one day. But love – the power of God, the oxygen of the Body of Christ – will never fail.

We can put too much emphasis on Spiritual gifts; they can sometimes be like toys. God gives them to build us up and that is their purpose. Our goal, when we come together is to meet with God; to love him and to hear him express his love to us. Paul says: (v.11) *when I became a man I put away childish things*.

Let us not be distracted by what can sometimes seem impressive displays of the supernatural; let us keep our focus on him and hear what he is saying to his people: *the greatest … is love* (v.13); love is (Chapter 12: 31) a more excellent way.

The Prophetic Gifts (1 Corinthians 14)

> *Pursue love, and desire spiritual gifts, but especially that you may prophesy. ² For he who speaks in a tongue does not speak to men but to God, for no one understands him; however, in the spirit he speaks mysteries. 3 But he who prophesies speaks edification and exhortation and comfort to men. ⁴ He who speaks in a tongue edifies himself, but he who prophesies edifies the church. ⁵ I wish you all spoke with tongues, but even more that you prophesied; for he who prophesies is greater than he who speaks with*

> *tongues, unless indeed he interprets, that the church may receive edification.*

(1 Corinthians 14: 1-5)

Paul reminds the church to pursue love and desire spiritual gifts, which briefly summarises the message of Chapters 13 and 12, but this is *especially that you may prophesy.*

Prophecy is a real hot potato in many congregations. There are those who see prophecy as equal to – or even higher than – the Bible in their conversation with God; this is dangerous. There are more conservative groups who are suspicious of it and seek to qualify and evaluate everything with great care. This is right (see v. 29), but underneath the caution is the fear that 'prophetic' utterances are likely to be attempts to manipulate, or even demonic attempts to spread lies and false teaching. Then there are many congregations who are unfamiliar with prophetic gifts and simply don't believe in them. I'm sure Paul faced much the same range of attitudes in the first century, but he is very clear that the Holy Spirit desires and intends to intervene directly and prophetically in our worship.

Rather than speaking in tongues, h*e who prophesies speaks edification, exhortation and comfort* (v.3), he continues: *I wish you all spoke with tongues, but even more that you prophesied … that the church may receive edification* (v.5).

Edification – 'building up' – is one of the principal works of the Holy Spirit in the church. We are built up into the Lord's holy temple through the presence of the Holy Spirit and the gifts that he has given us. Why would we presume to be able to do this without the enabling gifts?

The answer to both the over-reliance on prophecies and the fear of false or misguided prophecies is the discipline and order with which these gifts must be used. Our gifts are in our control (v.32). It isn't like a spooky séance where a medium goes into a trance to let the spirit speak. God isn't like that. He wants us in control of all our faculties at all times: *don't be drunk* (Ephesians 5: 18) *but be filled with the Spirit.* One of the themes running through these chapters in 1 Corinthians is that we should be mature in our faith and not like children.

Tongues and Interpretation

I wonder what sort of worship the Corinthians might have been used to that they assumed speaking in tongues without understanding would be a good thing to do.

> *Unless you utter by the tongue words easy to understand, how will it be known what is spoken? For you will be speaking into the air.*
>
> (1 Corinthians 14: 9)

Why would we go to a meeting and speak nonsense? (We may well ask!)

For followers of the 'mystery' religions speaking in tongues probably indicated the presence of the god or spirit they were attempting to call up – at least it showed that the worshipper was ecstatic and having a good time.

But Christian worship is different. *If I do not know the meaning of the language, I shall be a foreigner to him who speaks …* (v.11), in other words, we will have no fellowship; this will not build up the Body of Christ. Understanding is essential. Paul continues: *since you are zealous for spiritual gifts, let it be for the edification of the church* (v.12).

It's good to want to be 'spiritual' and to use Spiritual gifts in worship. This is why God gave them to us, but the focus must always be 'edification', on building up the body.

Order in Worship

> *Whenever you come together, each of you has a psalm, has a teaching, has a tongue, has a revelation, has an interpretation. Let all things be done for edification.* [27] *If anyone speaks in a tongue, let there be two or at the most three, each in turn, and let one interpret.* [28] *But if there is no interpreter, let him keep silent in church, and let him speak to himself and to God.* [29] *Let two or three prophets speak, and let the others judge.* [30] *But if anything is revealed to another who sits by, let the first keep silent.* [31] *For you can all prophesy one by one, that all may learn and all may be encouraged.* [32] *And the spirits of the prophets are subject to the prophets.* [33] *For God is not the author of confusion but of peace, as in all the churches of the saints.*
>
> *(1 Corinthians 14: 26-33)*

In responding to a chaotic situation, Paul has given us very clear guidelines for using spiritual gifts in our worship.

Firstly, in v.26 there is the expectation that everyone will come to worship with some contribution. In a time when so much of our worship experience is directed from the front, notice that some of these contributions are substantial, like teaching. It is necessary for someone to lead or convene the meeting, but God has made the Body of Christ to minister to itself. You come with a song, someone else with a passage of scripture, another person with a prophecy, and so on – and all of this works to build up the church. We speak and we listen to God by speaking and listening to each other.

Paul tells us that two or three people should speak in tongues (v.27) and someone should interpret. Tongues in a worship meeting should always be followed by an interpretation; we want to know that God is speaking but we need to understand what he is saying. Paul also says that no more than three people should speak in turn; the gifts are given to be used but they are tools; they must never get out of control. It's easy to get carried away, so the leader needs the understanding and confidence to move the service on when the time is right.

Where there is no-one able to interpret, tongue-speakers should be quiet and *commune with God* in private (v.28). This begs the question: how do they know?

If there is a person with a clearly identifiable gift of *interpretation* it's easy, but these things are often revealed by trial and error. God doesn't get upset when we sometimes experiment and get it wrong. If someone speaks in tongues, the congregation should pause and wait for the interpretation; the leader should gently encourage in case there is someone who is not quite sure if they have the interpretation or not. In the middle of a worship service, if a person feels they have something to say, it will probably be 'right' – and this will be confirmed by other people's witness. (There is no objective way to tell – but we'll know if it's correct.)

In this way we learn to communicate in the Spirit. We start with little steps and gradually build confidence. This growing spiritual confidence and trust in one another shows the edification Paul speaks of.

Let two or three prophets speak, and let the others judge (v.29). Interpretation of tongues and prophecy are very similar gifts. We want to hear two or three things either by interpretation or prophecy – it's a guideline, not a law, but any more than that can become confusing. It's helpful if these words are recorded or written down so that they can be judged or evaluated.

We have to take what the Holy Spirit says seriously. It isn't just a question of whether a word is *true* or *false* but that God is speaking to his people. He may be giving a simple word of encouragement, which doesn't need much qualification, or he may be giving insights crucial to how the church will grow and develop in the future. These need to be tested with Scripture and with other indicators. Spiritual gifts are not wallpaper or a weird soundscape to a worship service: we must *rightly divide the word of truth* (2 Timothy 2: 15). And we can be sure that nothing given by prophecy will contradict Scripture or cause hurt.

> *The spirits of the prophets are subject to the prophets. [33] For God is not the author of confusion but of peace, as in all the churches of the saints*
>
> *(vv.32, 33).*

When God gives us a spiritual gift it is in our control. He wants us to be mature in learning to handle it skilfully and to demonstrate his love and his grace in its use. Worship is not a crazy free-for-all or a mad rave, nor is it the solemn performance of an ancient rite: we are ministers in the presence of God, building one another up in faith and love while we honour and bless him.

Pictures

Many Old Testament prophets described vivid images, sometimes from real life, sometimes from highly surreal visions. Sometimes they delivered messages in plain language and used images as illustrations (Jeremiah 18: 1-4), and sometimes it can be very hard to be sure exactly what they meant (Ezekiel 1). People who see pictures like this are sometimes called seers – that is, they see things (see 1 Samuel 9: 8, 9).

Paul doesn't mention people seeing pictures in any of his teaching about spiritual gifts, but it seems to be quite a common thing. We should probably treat pictures in the same way as prophecies, that is, we should test them to see if they accord with scripture and what the Holy Spirit is saying in other ways and ensure that they are given in an orderly way.

As with all types of prophetic gift, the Holy Spirit speaks consistently and coherently to his church, not all at the same time or even in the same place, but always in a way that builds up the whole body. It's very rare (and possibly suspect) for a prophecy to be completely unique or unexpectedly 'new'.

Spiritual Gifts and Leading Worship

Some worship leaders, at the end of a song will say something like 'lift up your hearts to the Lord' and step back allowing others to sing or speak in tongues and to prophesy. This seamless transition requires the congregation to be used to prophetic worship and have the discipline to keep it orderly. Sometimes this can be led subtly through music and continue for extended periods; it can be very beautiful and form an intimate exchange through prayer and prophecy with the Holy Spirit.

It's more likely that the leader will need to create opportunities for 'open' worship during the service and encouraging people explicitly to share any word or picture that they may have.

Earnestly desire the best gifts.

(1 Corinthians 12: 31)

Discussion 12

How do you understand Spiritual Gifts?

- Why are they given?
- To whom are they given?

Give examples of when you have been aware of a 'word of knowledge' or 'word of wisdom'?

What role does the Gift of 'Healing' play in our worship?

Is it okay for healing to be the main focus of a meeting?

How can we make our worship 'prophetic'?

- Give examples of when you have used or witnessed this Gift in the context of leading worship.

Can (and should) singing in tongues be interpreted?

- How could this be done in practice?
- What is the difference between an 'interpretation' and a 'translation'?

How can spiritual gifts be abused?

- Is there space for anything in our gathering together that doesn't specifically build the church up?
- Is there space for anything in our lives at all that isn't spiritually edifying?

How important is it to enjoy worship?

Practically, how can you balance freedom in worship with doing everything 'decently and in order'?

13. "The Anointing that Breaks the Yoke"

> *And it shall come to pass in that day, that [the king of Assyria's] burden shall be taken away from off thy shoulder, and his yoke from off thy neck, and the yoke shall be destroyed because of the anointing [oil].*
>
> *(Isaiah 10:27 KJV)*

This verse needs some explanation.

One of the most-described incidents in the Old Testament (in 2 Kings 18-20; 2 Chronicles 29-32 and Isaiah 36-39) is the story of how king Hezekiah of the southern Israelite kingdom of Judah stood up against Sennacherib, king of the Assyrian empire.

Hezekiah had come to the throne as a young man, determined to restore the Temple and the worship of Yahweh, which had fallen away in the reign of his father. He succeeded in doing this – and everything went well until he refused to pay tax to the Assyrians. They invaded and destroyed the Judean city of Lachish, taking loot and slaves away into captivity. Next, they threatened Jerusalem itself and Hezekiah called on God for help, supported by the prophet Isaiah. God intervened and Sennacherib withdrew, only to be murdered by his sons shortly afterwards.

A *yoke* is a heavy wooden beam that goes between two horses or oxen if they are pulling a plough or a wagon; at times yokes have also been used to shackle prisoners to prevent them escaping. The heavy beam would be tied or shackled to a prisoner's neck and arms. The word has come to represent slavery and captivity, which – Isaiah says – would be broken because of the anointing.

***

We hear a lot of people in Pentecostal churches talking about the *anointing*. By this they mean (loosely) the action or presence of the Holy Spirit. If a person, song or thing is blessed by God or directed by the Holy Spirit it is said to be *anointed*. This view of the anointing is central to the teaching of some churches; it is the presence of God; the power of God; it is the authority of God: *Christ in you the hope of glory*. In this chapter I want to explore what this anointing is from Scripture and in particular how it can break the yoke of captivity. This is vital to us as we seek to live free and declare the freedom of God to others. Worship in God's holy place should be a place of unique freedom

> *Where the Spirit of the Lord is, there is liberty.*
>
> 2 Corinthians 3: 17

On the other hand, there are people in more traditional churches who have probably never heard the word used in this way and don't understand what it means, or perhaps they teach that there has only ever been one *Anointed One* – one *Christ* – and that anyone else claiming to be 'anointed' must be antichrist. This is confusing.

Anointing is a strange word anyway. What does it mean? What does the Bible say about it?

The word means 'smearing or rubbing with oil', like an 'ointment'. In Bible times, most people used olive oil like soap, so in a basic way everyone was anointed most of the time. That doesn't help much.

The Greek word *Khristos* (from which we get 'Christ') means 'anointed': *Iēsus Khristos* – Jesus, the Anointed One – meant absolutely nothing to people in Bible times who weren't Jews. Some Romans referred to him as *khrēstos*, which means 'useful' because that made more sense to them. To the Jews though, calling Jesus 'Christ' was like calling him God.

Why?

'Anointing' in the Old Testament

Priests and the Tabernacle
In the Old Testament, certain groups of people were anointed with specially prepared oil. Firstly, the priests who served in the Tabernacle were anointed to carry out holy duties:

> *Like a skilled incense maker, blend these ingredients to make a holy anointing oil.* [26] *Use this sacred oil to anoint the Tabernacle, the Ark of the Covenant,* [28] *[and all the other equipment used for worship] …* [29] *Consecrate them to make them absolutely holy. After this, whatever touches them will also become holy.*

> *[30] Anoint Aaron and his sons also, consecrating them to serve me as priests. [31] And say to the people of Israel, 'This holy anointing oil is reserved for me from generation to generation...'*
>
> *(Exodus 30: 25-31 NLT)*

(Remember the definition of 'holy' we used in chapter 4 – 'separate'.)

The oil was poured onto the fabric of the Tabernacle and the worship equipment to show that it was holy; the same oil was poured onto the head and the clothes of the priests. In a way the priests were being made part of the 'worship equipment' in the Tabernacle; neither they nor their stuff was allowed to mingle with 'the world outside'. Because of the special spices and other ingredients in this oil it was like perfume and was clearly distinguished from the normal oil they used for cooking or for any other purpose; its scent would have filled the tabernacle and seeped into the clothes of the priests. Generation after generation of priests were anointed in this way. It was a sign of their holiness – of their separation – and also of their special authority to speak to God and conduct worship on behalf of the people.

Kings

Secondly, the king was anointed to reign.

> *Then Samuel took a flask of oil and poured it on [Saul's] head, and kissed him and said: "Is it not because the LORD has anointed you commander over His inheritance?"*

(1 Samuel 1: 10)

Then Zadok the priest took a horn of oil from the tabernacle and anointed Solomon. And they blew the horn, and all the people said, "Long live King Solomon!"

(1 Kings 1: 39)

Two kings a generation apart: Saul and Solomon. Saul was Israel's first king. Although he started out well, he disobeyed God (1 Samuel 15) and was replaced by David whom Samuel anointed while Saul was still king (1 Samuel 16: 13). Saul declined in power and David became prominent, especially after killing the giant Goliath (1 Samuel 17); their relationship was difficult. Saul, envious of David's growing influence, set out with an army to kill him. On one of these occasions, David was able to ambush the sleeping king but refused to kill him saying: *The LORD forbid that I should stretch out my hand against the LORD'S anointed* (1 Samuel 26: 11).

David understood that even though Saul was a bad king and a personal threat, and that he was himself the rightful successor (anointed, indeed), Saul was holy – separated to God – and therefore David would not harm him. He respected Saul because he honoured God. Although Saul was conflicted and did a lot of evil things, he still carried God's anointing.

Solomon was king after David. In this case one of David's other sons, Adonijah had appointed himself king while David was on his deathbed. This was wrong on two counts: firstly, he had no right to appoint himself king (particularly since David had made it clear who should be king after him – it was an act of rebellion); secondly because without being anointed by God's servant he had no authority to be king. It was the anointing by Zadok that made Solomon king and separated him to God.

From this we see that priests and kings in Israel had a particular God-given authority placed on them by their anointing, which could not be removed or gained in any other way. The act of anointing with oil is only a symbol of this authority; the actual power came from God.

Kings and priests were two of the ways that God spoke to his people. The priest was the way for the people to come to God through sacrifices and the ordered worship of the Tabernacle; the kings were *commanders of the people* (1 Samuel 9: 16) to give physical assurance and protection and to provide leadership.

Anointing for both of these groups gave authority for their office and separated them for God's service.

Prophets

There is a third role in the Old Testament associated with anointing: the prophets. Samuel was the prophet who anointed Saul and later David as king; Nathan the prophet was present when Zadok anointed Solomon, however there is no record of prophets in the Old Testament being anointed, with two exceptions.

Unlike kings and priests who were anointed and served God before witnesses or in public, prophets were called in private. Often, we see them almost wrestling with God's Word on their own – as in the cases of Jonah (see Chapter 5) and Jeremiah, who argued with God about his calling (Jeremiah 1: 6). Micaiah is another example. He was a prophet in the time of Ahab, king of the northern kingdom of Israel.

> *Meanwhile, the messenger who went to get Micaiah said to him, "Look, all the prophets are promising victory for the king. Be sure that you agree with them and promise success."*
>
> *[14] But Micaiah replied, "As surely as the LORD lives, I will say only what the LORD tells me to say."*
>
> *(1 Kings 22: 13, 14)*

The other so-called 'prophets' were all declaring a great victory for king Ahab against the Arameans, but Micaiah refused to say anything except what God had told him to say, and his news, as it turned out, was very different from theirs.

Often prophets are called 'out of the blue' by God and don't have their authority given by someone else:

> *Then the word of the LORD came to me, saying:*
>
> *[5] "Before I formed you in the womb I knew you; before you were born I sanctified you; I ordained you a prophet to the nations."*
>
> *(Jeremiah 1: 4, 5)*

This is the source of their authority. Although kings and priests were ordained by God and had to serve him, they also served the people. Prophets were different: they took their words directly from God and delivered their messages exactly as he directed; they often lived away from other people; sometimes, like Micaiah or Jeremiah above, they were regarded as dangerous. Prophets often seem to serve as the king's conscience – especially when the king wasn't walking with God. In a way, the prophets were anointed by God himself.

There are two exceptions to this. Elisha was anointed for ministry as a prophet. In 1 Kings 19: 15-18, when Elijah is hiding in the mountains from Jezebel, he hears the word of God to anoint Elisha as prophet in his place (1 Kings 19: 16). The way this happened is odd because the term 'anoint' appears to be used metaphorically; Elijah's authority to prophesy appears to be transferred by his cloak rather than by actual anointing with oil (1 Kings 19: 19-21 and 2 Kings 2: 9-14). This is the first time that anointing is described like a spiritual gift – Elijah's prophetic gift and ministry transfers to Elisha in much the same way as the gifts of the Holy Spirit we discussed in the previous chapter.

Secondly, in 2 Samuel 15: 27, Zadok, who was anointed as a priest is also called a seer, a kind of prophet, and it is he who anoints Solomon as king. It is his role as a prophet that gives him the authority to anoint the new king, not his anointing as a priest.

The symbolic meaning of anointing

> *Behold, how good and how pleasant it is for brethren to dwell together in unity!*
>
> *² It is like the precious oil upon the head, running down on the beard, the beard of Aaron, running down on the edge of his garments.*
>
> *³ It is like the dew of Hermon, descending upon the mountains of Zion; for there the LORD commanded the blessing—Life forevermore.*
>
> *(Psalm 133)*

The image here is of Moses pouring oil onto the head of Aaron, the first High Priest, and of the oil running down his beard and edges of his priestly robes. This, says the writer, is like the dew on Mount Hermon. Hermon is a high mountain in the north of Israel on the Syrian border; this Hermon-dew is also falling on Mount Zion in Jerusalem where the Temple would later be. Now, Moses actually anointed Aaron at Mount Sinai in the south of the country, so this short Psalm is showing how the whole of the nation of Israel is united in space and in time by the anointing of Aaron, the first priest. The anointing oil was a way of showing that the authority and blessing of God was in Israel through the Law, represented by Aaron.

This blessing of God flowed downwards through the anointing, through the kings and priests and from the prophets to the rest of the people. Adonijah was unable to become king without it. It shows the order that God put at the centre of his people through the Law.

This helps us to understand the verse at the beginning of this chapter:

> *It shall come to pass in that day, that [the king of Assyria's] burden shall be taken away from off thy shoulder, and his yoke from off thy neck, and the yoke shall be destroyed because of the anointing [oil].*
>
> (Isaiah 10: 27 KJV)

This *anointing*[16] that will break the yoke of slavery is God's promise of blessing and rescue to his people (Deuteronomy 28: 7) demonstrated in the presence of the king, the priests and the whole nation serving him.

Hezekiah's struggle to return Judah to worshipping Yahweh and to break away from Assyrian domination is told in 2 Kings 18-20; 2 Chronicles 29-32 and Isaiah 36-39. He is successful eventually through returning to the Spiritual authority of the Law. It is the *anointing* – the renewed Spiritual authority: the renewed holiness of the priests and Levites, the rededication of the temple and the re-institution of the Passover, as well as the godly advice of Isaiah the prophet – that breaks the power of the Assyrians.

The *anointing* also represents the presence of God's blessing in the land brought about by Hezekiah's obedience.

The Messiah – the Anointed One

> *Why do the nations rage and the people plot a vain thing?*
>
> *² The kings of the earth set themselves, and the rulers take counsel together,*
>
> *Against the LORD and against His Anointed, saying,*
>
> *³ "Let us break Their bonds in pieces and cast away Their cords from us."*
>
> *(Psalm 2: 1-3)*

In this Psalm, the nations of the earth gather themselves to threaten Yahweh and his Anointed One. Our first impression is that the Anointed person it refers to (v.2) is the king – King David – who wrote this Psalm. It would be natural for him to claim the protection of Yahweh in this way.

But as the Psalm continues, we see that David can't be writing about himself:

> *He who sits in the heavens shall laugh; the LORD shall hold them in derision.*
>
> *⁵ Then He shall speak to them in His wrath, and distress them in His deep displeasure:*
>
> *⁶ "Yet I have set My King on My holy hill of Zion."*

> *[7] "I will declare the decree: the LORD has said to Me, 'You are My Son, today I have begotten You. [8] Ask of Me, and I will give You the nations for Your inheritance, and the ends of the earth for Your possession. [9] You shall break them with a rod of iron; You shall dash them to pieces like a potter's vessel.'"*

(Psalm 2: 4-9)

Yahweh laughs at the nations, at the kings of the earth who come to threaten his people. He says: *I have set My King on My holy hill of Zion* (v.6), we still might be thinking that he means David, but then he says: *the LORD has said to Me, 'You are My Son, today I have begotten You* (v.7). This can't possibly be David.

Yahweh's Anointed One is his begotten[17] Son (see John 1: 14; Hebrews 1), and he will reign victorious over all the earth.

> *My heart is overflowing with a good theme; I recite my composition concerning the King; My tongue is the pen of a ready writer.*

(Psalm 45: 1)

Psalm 45 isn't by David but by a group of Levites called 'the Sons of Korah' who wrote many Psalms of praise. The writer starts by saying that he's going to write about the King, possibly David or Solomon, we might think.

The next few verses are a beautiful description of this King and how God (it doesn't say Yahweh) has blessed him, and then he says in verses 6 and 7:

> *Your throne, O God, is forever and ever; a sceptre of righteousness is the sceptre of Your kingdom. ⁷ You love righteousness and hate wickedness; therefore God, Your God, has anointed You with the oil of gladness more than Your companions.*

(Psalm 45: 6, 7)

It says that the King has been anointed by God with the oil of gladness more than his companions. We know who anointed David and Solomon to be king. But more surprising – more shocking to the Jews – is the idea that this Psalm is really about God himself. *Your throne, O God, is forever and ever* (v.6). God is himself anointed 'by God'.

We know that only priests, kings and very rarely prophets are anointed, and that this anointing demonstrates God's authority. This is God's promise to the Jewish people that he was going to send an Anointed One (in Hebrew, *Messiah*; in Greek *Christ*) to be a king not just over Israel but the entire world; that he would be his begotten Son – and that he would in fact be God himself.

So, we can see why the Jews got upset about Jesus being called Christ or Messiah. Nevertheless, Jesus Christ is God's Anointed. He is the Jews' Messiah and he is the only begotten Son of God (John 3: 16). The New Testament makes it clear that he is a *prophet* (Luke 7: 16), a *priest* (Hebrews 4: 14) and a *king* (Revelation 19: 16). He fills all the Old Testament anointed ministries.

Jesus 'breaks the yoke'

Returning to the verse at the beginning of this chapter, Jesus himself breaks the yoke of oppression.

> *Because God's children are human beings — made of flesh and blood — the Son also became flesh and blood. For only as a human being could he die, and only by dying could he break the power of the devil, who had the power of death.* [15] *Only in this way could he set free all who have lived their lives as slaves to the fear of dying.*
>
> (Hebrews 2: 14, 15 NLT)

People today aren't too bothered about the king of Assyria. He was nasty but he's long gone and been replaced in their time by other tyrants as bad and worse. The real 'tyrant' now, what people dread most in life, is the fear of death; their own death and the death of their loved ones. And if death itself doesn't seem a threat right now, then there are other things that lead in that direction; things that threaten, disempower and disable us: poverty, sickness, loss, being bullied or manipulated by others – the effects of sin that lead inevitably to death.

Jesus said: *The thief does not come except to steal, and to kill, and to destroy. I have come that they may have life, and that they may have it more abundantly* (John 10: 10). Jesus brought love, joy, peace; he brought hope, salvation and the forgiveness of sins when he laid his life down on the cross. Jesus Christ is the Word of God in bodily form, the fulness of God revealed. He is the centre of our worship; he is the object of our praise and our affection. We praise him!

The 'anointing' in the New Testament

> *Then, six days before the Passover, Jesus came to Bethany, where Lazarus was who had been dead, whom He had raised from the dead. [2] There they made Him a supper; and Martha served, but Lazarus was one of those who sat at the table with Him. [3] Then Mary took a pound of very costly oil of spikenard, anointed the feet of Jesus, and wiped His feet with her hair. And the house was filled with the fragrance of the oil.*
>
> *[4] But one of His disciples, Judas Iscariot, Simon's son, who would betray Him, said, [5] "Why was this fragrant oil not sold for three hundred denarii and given to the poor?" [6] This he said, not that he cared for the poor, but because he was a thief, and had the money box; and he used to take what was put in it.*
>
> *[7] But Jesus said, "Let her alone; she has kept this for the day of My burial. [8] For the poor you have with you always, but Me you do not have always."*
>
> *(John 12: 1-8)*

This is a different kind of anointing because it says more about the one who gave it than about Jesus who received it. Jesus was the Anointed One of God; his authority was and is absolute so nothing that Mary did could change that or add to it.

When Judas complained about the waste, Jesus answers that she was anointing him *for his burial*; the last person Mary anointed in this way was her brother, which would have been heart-breaking for her. When Jesus visited them (just before he raised Lazarus from the dead) Martha met him and even challenged him (John 11: 20, 21), but Mary stayed inside; she is absent from the rest of the story of Lazarus' resurrection. She was grieving.

So, Mary must still have been in a state of emotional turmoil at this meal. She had watched her brother become sick and die while Jesus delayed his arrival. It must have seemed cruel, and yet she knew Jesus and had sat at his feet while he taught (Luke 10: 38-42). She hadn't been able to face him during his visit to the tomb, even as he brought her brother back from the dead and changed everything. She must have been emotionally exhausted but needed some way to express the pressure of love, loss, grief and gratitude that was building in her both for Lazarus and for Jesus.

And then there were wider concerns that added to her stress – some people were now trying to kill both Lazarus and Jesus (John 12: 9-11), which seems absurd to us but to Mary added a layer of hurt and insult to the injury she was already dealing with. Also, there was a house full of people when she really needed some time with her brother.

We can see these things. But we still don't really know what was in her mind – whether she had an insight into Jesus' death or not – but it is clear what was in her heart. John simply tells us that *she took a pound of very costly oil of spikenard, anointed the feet of Jesus, and wiped His feet with her hair* (v.3). If this is the same incident that is recorded in Mark 14: 3, she actually broke the jar and dumped the whole contents on Jesus' feet. Judas, horrified, complains that this was worth a large amount of money, about a year's wages. Again, we don't know exactly what this represented to Mary, perhaps it was set aside for her wedding, but it was extremely precious, something that she had been keeping.

At that time, spikenard was only found in a few valleys in the Himalayas; its roots were crushed to produce a richly fragrant oil. As we have seen previously, it is mentioned in one other book in the Bible:

> Him: *[9] I have compared you, my love, to a company of horses in Pharaoh's chariots.*
> *[10] Your cheeks are lovely with ornaments, your neck with chains of gold. 11 We will make you ornaments of gold with studs of silver.*
>
> Her: *[12] While the king is at his table, my spikenard sends forth its fragrance. [13] A bundle of myrrh is my beloved to me, and he shall lie all night between my breasts. [14] My beloved is to*

me as a cluster of henna blooms in the vineyards of En Gedi.

(Song of Solomon 1: 9-14)

This is a picture of romance, of courtship, of seduction almost; a picture of Christ and his bride, described hundreds of years before Jesus. Mary's ointment is no subtle hint of perfume; it's the heavy fragrance of incense. It's as if Mary is taking her most treasured aspiration, her marriage, and giving it to Jesus. It is not a romantic proposal but a sacrifice. She is figuratively laying her life down at Jesus' feet.

Spikenard was also used in the preparation of the ketoret – the special incense burned on the incense altar in the Sanctuary. As the house was *filled with the fragrance of the oil* (v.3), it must have brought to mind the burning of the holy incense in the Temple.

Judas was right in a way. The perfume could have been sold; it would have been sensible for her to have made a donation to Jesus' ministry. But Mary isn't being *sensible*. She is overwhelmed with love, gratitude and worship; she wipes her hair in the oil to rub it into Jesus feet, so she anoints and abases herself at the same time as worshipping Jesus.

In Mary we see love, abandonment in worship and the sacrifice of her most precious possession; the perfume itself speaks of love and intimacy, and of the most holy place in the sanctuary. Mary is a model for how we should come before God in worship.

Our anointing

> *However, when He, the Spirit of truth, has come, He will guide you into all truth; for He will not speak on His own authority, but whatever He hears He will speak; and He will tell you things to come. [14] He will glorify Me, for He will take of what is Mine and declare it to you. [15] All things that the Father has are Mine. Therefore I said that He will take of Mine and declare it to you.*

(John 16: 13-15)

We've looked so far at what anointing meant in the Old Testament, especially in the ordination of priests and kings and as something that represented God's authority in the nation of Israel. We started with the promise that the power of the Assyrian king would be destroyed *because of the anointing*. We've seen that Jesus Christ is the Anointed One, the *only begotten Son of God* who is prophesied to rule over the whole world. He also has broken the power of the fear of death – worse than any evil ruler. Then in Mary, we saw anointing in a different way, as worship. *Your name is ointment poured forth*, says the woman in Song of Solomon 1: 3. In Elisha we saw the word 'anointing' used symbolically to show the transfer of the gift of prophecy from Elijah to Elisha, which he does with his cloak rather than with oil.

In John 16 Jesus promises his disciples another Comforter – the Holy Spirit – who would come to them when he had departed. Jesus says that this Comforter, the Spirit of Truth *will guide you into all tru*th (v.13).

That's a big promise – it's the promise, made by Jesus right at the beginning, that his church would be guided by his own voice. *He will not speak on His own authority, but whatever He hears He will speak* (v.13) ... *He will take of what is Mine and declare it to you* (v. 14). In other words, the wisdom of Jesus, who is the Word of God, is at the heart of his church.

Some have said that this is intended only for the disciples, the first Apostles of the church; that this promise is not for everyone. But I don't agree. John says in his first letter, right at the very end of the Apostolic Age:

> *But you have an anointing from the Holy One, and you know all things.*

(1 John 2: 20)

showing the fulfilment of the words of Jesus in John 16.

How are we to read this? It's important to get it right because these can be dangerous words if they are misunderstood. We can imagine cult-leaders – Jim Jones, David Koresh and the like – taking hold of words like these and using them to manipulate the vulnerable. But let's think about the truth that stands behind the words; the theology, if you will.

We *have an anointing from the Holy One* and we *know all things*.

But there are clearly many things about which we know nothing! And a lot of what we do know is either irrelevant or rubbish. Knowing who scored the winning goal of the 1974 F.A. Cup Final isn't very helpful, and as Donald Rumsfeld helpfully pointed out[18], *we don't know what we don't know.*

John isn't talking about the ability to reproduce facts or even to develop good teaching; he isn't even talking about correct doctrine – though these things are important. We are human, our minds are tiny, and we only understand about God what he shows us. Jesus said: *I am … the truth* (John 14: 6). The *anointing from the Holy One* is about knowing him.

Jesus promised his Spirit – the Holy Spirit – to be our Comforter, the one who makes us strong. The Greek word for Comforter is *paraklētos*, it means one who speaks or calls beside us – like a counsellor or advocate. Jesus said that his Spirit would be with us, also in us (John 14: 17). Jesus himself is with us by his Spirit and he speaks to us and we can know him. *Though I have the gift of prophecy, and understand all mysteries and all knowledge… but have not love, I am nothing* (1 Corinthians 13: 2). Jesus is love perfected.

> *Do not worry about how or what you should speak. For it will be given to you in that hour what you should speak; [20] for it is not you who speak, but the Spirit of your Father who speaks in you.*
>
> *(Matthew 10: 19, 20, see also Luke 12: 11)*

Jesus said that the Holy Spirit will *take what is mine and declare it to you* (John 16: 15). When God created the universe, Jesus was there: he was – is – the Word that comes out of the Father's mouth – out of his heart. He is our wisdom (1 Corinthians 1: 30). We might at this moment be very far from possessing all knowledge and all wisdom; but we have within us the Holy Spirit, who is the anointing from the Holy One, who is the source of all knowledge and wisdom.

Sometimes we are perplexed and baffled by what is in front of us – but the answer to our confusion isn't very often 'the answer' to a particular question (if that makes any sense). The way the church – the Body of Christ – works is that we can help to build each other up in the way we explored in the previous chapter.

> *The anointing which you have received from Him abides in you, and you do not need that anyone teach you; but as the same anointing teaches you concerning all things, and is true, and is not a lie, and just as it has taught you, you will abide in Him.*
>
> (1 John 2: 27)

It often happens when we are at prayer with others that another person will pray using words that speak directly to us, or perhaps they will be given a word of prophecy or a picture that makes a connection with something that was already in our minds, so God builds us up. As we abide in him, he will make us into the best and most complete people that it's possible for us to be because his Word abides in us and we do this learning and growing together.

This is what our anointing is. It doesn't come through ceremony or the pouring of oil on our heads; nor does it come through any special learning or initiation. If we are in Christ, then he is in us through the Holy Spirit; he breaks the yoke inside and releases us from the things that control and limit; he repairs the damage done to us by our past; he breaks the influence of poor self-esteem and unhelpful behaviours; he gives us wisdom and the ability to make healthy relationships. He gives us the ability to start again – to be *transformed by the renewing of our minds* (Romans 12: 2).

The anointing *abides in us*. We don't have to pray for it at the beginning of a service or wait for it to arrive. The Holy Spirit of God, his authority and Word within us will never leave us or forsake us.

Our Authority

> *You are a chosen generation, a royal priesthood, a holy nation, His own special people, that you may proclaim the praises of Him who called you out of darkness into His marvellous light.*
>
> *(1 Peter 2: 9)*
>
> *[Jesus Christ] has made us kings and priests to His God and Father, to Him be glory and dominion forever and ever. Amen.*
>
> *(Revelation 1: 6)*

Peter calls the Christians in Asia Minor *a royal priesthood and a holy nation*; John in his opening comments in the book of Revelation calls us *kings and priests*. How does that work?

These verses show us that the gift that God has given us is the same authority that was given to the priests, kings and prophets in the Old Testament.

These offices were very narrow: kings and priests served in specific ways; the fact that they were anointed – made holy – meant that they were unable to live ordinary lives and 'rub shoulders' with the world. They were physically separate from the rest of the people. Prophets, too, held a narrow mandate. Often what we know about an Old Testament Prophet is one word, sometimes called their burden from the Lord – the single message that defines their life and ministry.

Our mission is different. We are told to *go into the world* (Matthew 28: 19), not to withdraw from it. Our anointing does not separate us physically – but it separates us all the same.

> *Present your bodies a living sacrifice, holy, acceptable to God, which is your reasonable service.* [2] *And do not be conformed to this world, but be transformed by the renewing of your mind, that you may prove what is that good and acceptable and perfect will of God.*
>
> (Romans 12: 1, 2)

If we want to be useful to God and to his people, we must be different. Paul says: *present your bodies a living sacrifice, holy, acceptable to God, which is your reasonable service* (v.1), which is the same as the priests had to do when they were anointed; they were made *absolutely holy* (Exodus 30: 29 NLT). We cannot be different from this, and the Holy Spirit will bring holiness about within us. As we make the decision, day by day, to live holy and not to be conformed to this world, he will do the rest and transform us by renewing our minds – by taking our focus and our ambitions away from the things that would naturally occupy our thoughts, and refocusing us on his Word (see Psalm 19: 7-14).

The Old Testament priests were a kind of gateway to God for ordinary people. They enabled people to repent of their sin and become right with God through making the correct sacrifices. Jesus – the ultimate priest – sacrificed himself and removed the obstacle of sin once and for all, but most people still experience the effects of sin in their lives; they have no experience of God and no message of hope. We have the mission to make this message known and to enable people to meet with God for themselves – and this is a priestly role.

We've seen that Jesus Christ is the ultimate King – *King of kings and Lord of lords* (Revelation 19: 16) – and that he is destined to reign over the entire earth because he's the Messiah, the Anointed One (Psalm 2). He is *heir of all things* (Hebrews 1: 2). All of creation will one day return to him because he made it in the first place. It is his by right. In Romans 8: 12-17 Paul describes us as sons, and therefore *heirs* of God. Some modern translations slip over 'sons' and put 'children' instead because they want to include everyone, but this is missing the point. Regardless of our particular gender[19], he has made us sons and therefore *heirs*[20] with Christ.

This is hard to imagine. When Jesus reigns as sovereign on earth, in some way, we will reign with him.

> *Beloved, now we are [sons] of God; and it has not yet been revealed what we shall be, but we know that when He is revealed, we shall be like Him, for we shall see Him as He is.*
>
> (1 John 3: 2)

This is the end-point of what the Holy Spirit is doing in us – in the Body of Christ. He is forming us into the likeness of Christ.

The Anointing in Worship

In the previous chapter we looked in detail at how the Holy Spirit works in the Body of Christ to build up, to heal and to encourage – to *edify*. And we've looked here at the authority God gives us through the Holy Spirit to speak his Word, to lead others to him and – in the end – to reign with him.

When we meet together Jesus is present with us. It's not like he's 'the unseen guest' in some mysterious way, but he lives in us, so we bring him with us. We don't have to strive to achieve the presence of God or to be extra-especially holy. It doesn't matter how we dress (within reason); if we're talented singers or if we sound like Elisha's bears.

The anointing is not something that comes with a shivery feeling or sweaty palms, or when it's really quiet in a prayer time; nor is it introduced with an E5 chord or with a powerful Spirit-inspired message.

The Holy Spirit draws us together because He – God – wants to spend time with us together; to speak to us and teach us. And he loves it when we open our hearts to worship him. It isn't about what we feel or don't feel. He knows that we have real needs and that we struggle under various kinds of oppression – of *yoke*.

For us it isn't the king of Assyria who makes threatening noises, but one way or another, the effects of sin leech the life from us all. Often, we're tired of fighting battles – but being in the presence of the Holy Spirit in one another lifts us. He gives us wisdom to speak, to sing, to heal, and the authority to speak with his Word. We don't need qualifications to do this because he has made us kings and priests to himself. The anointing of Christ in us breaks the yoke of bondage to the world.

Discussion 14

Mary of Bethany's expression of worship in John 12 is extreme. She is completely devoted in her worship of Jesus.

- How can we help our brothers and sisters to achieve this level of devotion in their worship?
- Think of some words or phrases that you associate with this kind of 'devoted' worship.
- Are there any songs that speak to you of devoted worship?

How do you understand 'anointing'?

How can you apply this understanding to worship?

Prepare 15 or 20 minutes of corporate worship.

14. Worship and Mission

In the last section of Chapter 2, we saw first Isaiah and then the eleven disciples worshipping and then being commissioned to 'go'. Earlier in that chapter we saw, in Psalm 95: 7, 8, God saying, *Today, if you will hear His voice, do not harden your hearts...* When we encounter God in worship, we must expect him to invite a response of some kind.

We cannot enter the presence of God and remain untouched, and God calls us for a purpose. In the case of Isaiah, when he is broken by his apprehension of the presence of God and his unworthiness, God cleanses him and commissions him. And this commissioning has two parts in Isaiah 6: 8: *whom shall I send? And who will go for us?* We noted the double-meaning of this; God is seeking a servant and also an accomplice.

In Matthew 28, on the hilltop in Galilee, just before Jesus' ascension into heaven, the disciples *worshipped him*, though it says that *some doubted*. How are we to understand that? Many of them would not have understood what was happening; they may have been confused or sceptical. But in what sense did they *worship*?

They acknowledged that Jesus had conquered death. They had seen him cruelly crucified, speared and laid in a tomb – and then return to life again. It was one thing for Jesus to raise Jairus' daughter and the widow of Nain's son, or even to call Lazarus out of the tomb after four days. It was quite something else to raise himself from the dead. The man standing before them had demonstrated that he had personal authority that was greater than the laws of nature and had reversed the Fall. 'You shall not surely die', Satan had sneered at the woman. Now Jesus had proved it true, at Satan's expense.

Their worship would have been to acknowledge this.

With this knowledge also comes the realisation of their own failing. One of their number had betrayed him, another had denied him in his darkest hour; all of them in one way or another (with the possible exception of John) had turned their back on him. None had fully recognised his Messiahship or its implications. With Isaiah they might have said: Woe is me for I am undone! Then Jesus declared what they could already see:

> *All authority has been given to me in heaven and on earth. [19] Go therefore...*
>
> *(Matthew 28: 18, 19)*

Let's start this chapter by reiterating that when we worship, we enter God's holy place. We deliberately place ourselves in his way so that he will always speak to us. He will say something that amounts to:

> *Today, if you will hear His voice, do not harden your hearts ...*
>
> *(Psalm 95: 7, 8)*

He will say:

> *Whom shall I send, and who will go for Us?*

The test of worship is its fruit. If what you're doing doesn't naturally lead on to mission, it isn't worship.

A Personal Journey

As someone who is deeply convinced that everybody needs to hear the good news about Jesus and can follow him, I have often struggled with the confidence to share my faith. I had the sense that something was wrong.

I have learned what should have been obvious, that God doesn't call everybody to respond in the same way. Frankly, it's not everyone's job to knock on doors, and if that isn't your thing, then – seriously – don't do it. You're likely to do harm and you're probably going to get in the way of someone who really has been gifted in that way.

Nevertheless…

Jesus' commission is for everyone
So how do we all fit in? How do people like us obey Jesus' commission to make disciples – when they lack confidence and feel that they have no appropriate skills or abilities?

Jesus doesn't give us many commands, but his words to the apostles at the end of Matthew's and Mark's gospels are very clear.

> *Go therefore and make disciples of all the nations*
>
> (Matthew 28: 19)

> *Go into all the world and preach the gospel to every creature.*
>
> *(Mark 16: 15)*

Were these words intended just for the eleven remaining apostles? The book of Acts shows us that this isn't the case. Throughout it, many people – men and women – are reported actively sharing the hope that they have in Christ. So, we have a mandate, indeed we have the full authority of God to preach the gospel, to tell the good news about Jesus and to make disciples to him.

Is it possible even for introverts like us to play a full part in the mission of the church? It is – and indeed, we must.

> *There are diversities of gifts, but the same Spirit.*
> *[5] There are differences of ministries, but the same Lord. [6] And there are diversities of activities, but it is the same God who works all in all. [7] But the manifestation of the Spirit is given to each one for the profit of all.*
>
> 1 Corinthians 12: 4-7

Paul goes on to elaborate a list – as we saw in chapter 12. God gives different gifts to different people, and different degrees of faith (Romans 12: 3).

The call of God, the command to Go, is an integral part of worship. We approach him, he speaks with us and challenges us; *today, if you hear my voice, do not harden your hearts.* He calls us to respond. 'Go,' he says to Isaiah and his disciples on the mountain; 'Send me,' is the response. He commissions us.

As we move in obedience to his voice, he directs us and equips us to serve him effectively. Our service is not in 'doing what seems to be necessary', or even in doing what the pastor directs, but in following the inner prompting of the Holy Spirit as we spend time in his presence. So, we must not feel constrained to undertake 'missional' activities out of some sort of obligation but listen to him without hardness of heart as he prompts us to 'Go'; he will direct us in a way that is right and fruitful for us.

> *Take my hands and let them move*
> *At the impulse of Thy love;*
> *Take my feet and let them be*
> *Swift and beautiful for Thee.*
>
> *(Frances Ridley Havergal)*

This chapter is about *mission* as a response to worship.

What is Mission?

Some words.

The Latin word *missio*, from which we get 'mission' means 'send', 'throw' or 'dismiss'. An *emissarius* was a Roman spy, from which we get an *emissary* – a messenger. Other modern words derived from it are *emission*, something 'given off', perhaps in a car exhaust; *transmission* is passing something along. A *missive* is a letter, and *dismissal* is sending someone away. So, mission is to do with sending or being sent from one place to another.

There is a similarity in meaning between the Latin word *emissarius* and the Greek word *apostolos*, from which we get 'apostle'. Both are sent out with a purpose by a higher authority.

Nowadays we still use the word mission to express purpose. Companies have 'mission statements' that summarise their aims; we might say that we are 'on a mission' if we are being very purposeful about something. So, when we discuss our Christian *mission*, we're talking about our purpose in Christ. Why are we here? Why are we doing what we do? When we worship, God shares his heart with us; he tells us what his purpose for us is. He says, 'Go'. What will our response be?

God's Mission

Sending is in the nature of God. We've already discussed how God sends people, but sending is part of God's very essence.

The Father sends the Son

> *I have not spoken on My own authority; but the Father who sent Me gave Me a command, what I should say and what I should speak.*

> (John 12: 49)

> *God did not send His Son into the world to condemn the world, but that the world through Him might be saved.*
>
> *(John 3: 17)*

Jesus does not speak with his own authority but with the authority of the Father who sent him. His mission is to save the world. He is also called the 'apostle ... of our confession' (Hebrews 3: 1).

The Father and the Son send the Holy Spirit

> *But when the Helper comes, whom I shall send to you from the Father, the Spirit of truth who proceeds from the Father, He will testify of Me.*
>
> *(John 15: 26)*

The Holy Spirit is also sent with a purpose. Like Jesus, he originates with the Father but comes at the prompting of the Son. What is his mission? To testify of Jesus.

> *No one can say that Jesus is Lord except by the Holy Spirit.*
>
> *(1 Corinthians 12: 3).*

The Son sends the church – us

> *Jesus said to them again, "Peace to you! As the Father has sent Me, I also send you."*
>
> *(John 20: 21)*

The Father sends Jesus, his Son; the Father and Jesus send the Holy Spirit. Jesus sends us out into the world *in the name of the Father, the Son and the Holy Spirit* (Matthew 28: 19). What an amazing privilege it is to be included in the innate *sending* nature of God!

This is important because it shows us something about God's character. John 3: 17 states that God sent his Son to save the world. God is a redeemer. He wants to rescue us because he loves us.

When God introduces himself to Moses in the burning bush, he says:

> *I have surely seen the oppression of my people who are in Egypt, and have heard their cry because of their taskmasters, for I know their sorrows. So I have come down to deliver them out of the hand of the Egyptians ... Come now, therefore, and I will send you to Pharaoh that you may bring My people, the children of Israel, out of Egypt.*
>
> *(Exodus 3: 7, 8, 10)*

God has seen and heard and understood the mess the people are in; now he has come to send Moses on a mission to rescue them. Of course, he could have just 'smitten' the Egyptians anyway, but he needed to give Pharaoh the chance to get things right. So, he sent Moses – a man who understood him and spoke his language – a man, as it were, with *like passions* (Acts 14: 15).

Jonah understood this and it was the reason he disobeyed when God told him to go to Nineveh. He didn't want Nineveh to be saved, he would rather they all died in their sins.

God said:

> *Arise, go to Nineveh, that great city, and cry out against it; for their wickedness has come up before me.*
>
> *(Jonah 1: 2)*

And a little later…

> *Should I not pity Nineveh, that great city, in which are more than one hundred and twenty thousand persons who cannot discern between their right hand and their left.*
>
> *(Jonah 4: 11)*

All these accounts in the Old Testament point forward to what is to come. God's ultimate rescue mission, not just to save his 'chosen people' but the whole of humankind.

> *God so loved the world that He gave His only begotten Son, that whoever believes in Him should not perish but have everlasting life.*
>
> *(John 3: 16)*

Greater than Jonah; greater than Moses. God *sends* His own Word into the world as a man (John 1: 14) with a very precise mission to reveal the compassion and love of God in the world, and by it to bring about salvation. Because God sent his son, we are saved.

And so he also sends us (John 20: 21). Our mission is different from Jesus'. He came to lay his life down as a ransom and to be the sacrifice that God's righteousness demanded as the penalty for sin. We can't do that – and we don't need to because Jesus completed it. Our mission is to declare the done deal.

Where Moses, Jonah and the others were looking forward to a distant hope that must have seemed insubstantial at times, we can look back on the cross and know that it is real. It is a historical fact, and in that time and that place God reconciled the world to himself.

> *God was in Christ reconciling the world to Himself, not imputing their trespasses to them, and has committed to us the word of reconciliation.*
>
> *(2 Corinthians 5: 19)*

'And he has committed to us the word of reconciliation.'

This is not just something that we do. It is what we are. The Holy Spirit, whom God the Father and the Son send, lives inside us. In Christ, we are a new creation, made new; no longer in the pattern of the corrupted world but transformed from the inside out. *Born again*, Peter tells us, *of an incorruptible seed*.

This word of reconciliation is part of our nature. It's as if God has written it into our DNA.

We discussed in Chapter 5 how Jonah was effective as an evangelist on the storm-struck ship despite himself. All he did, in the middle of his deliberate disobedience, was to answer honestly when the terrified sailors asked him questions. In Matthew 5: 13 and 14, Jesus tells his assembled disciples:

You are the salt of the earth

You are the light of the world

Therefore, he says, behave in ways that use your saltiness and help your light to shine. If you choose to hide your light under a bucket – or in the hold of a ship – it will still be light, but it won't be useful.

(How can you lose your salty flavour? It's chemically impossible of course, but you can allow yourself to get contaminated by worldly thinking and perceptions. If you throw a handful of sand with a bit of salt into your stew, you'll think it's *lost its savour*.)

Jesus sends us into the world as the bearers of his word of reconciliation. Our mission is not to do the reconciling. He did that. It is simply to deliver the message.

In Isaiah's vision, God spoke two questions into the court of heaven:

Whom shall I send,

And who will go for Us?

Apart from the seraphim, we don't know who else is there, but we can imagine God addressing a vast host of heavenly beings (as in Revelation 4 and 5), the words are not apparently directed towards Isaiah. God is looking for a messenger to *send*: 'Whom shall I send?'

But God's emissary is not a mere cypher or a slave; a mouthpiece to reel off what God says. He undertakes the task of his own volition.

'Who will go for us?'

Isaiah grabs the opportunity boldly: *'Here I am, send me.'*

God sends different messengers with different messages. Gabriel, who visits Zachariah in Luke 1: 19 is a pure servant – he is an angel.

> *I am Gabriel, who stands in the presence of God, and was sent to speak to you and bring you these glad tidings.*

His entire existence is to stand in the presence of God and wait for a message like a footman in a stately home. In this case, a human messenger would not do. God intervened directly at the most sacred moment of Zachariah's life as a priest as he burned incense in the Holy Place. Gabriel's motives or his character are irrelevant.

But this is not the case with us. Often those who God calls answer him with human weakness. God engages in a long discussion from Exodus 3: 12 to 4: 17 about the various qualifications and assurances that Moses needs to be sure he is on the right track. In Jeremiah 1: 1-10, God calls Jeremiah and he answers with an excuse: *I cannot speak for I am a youth* (Jeremiah 4: 6). And God answers with assurances about how he will put words in his mouth. And Jonah – who we have already seen –

answered God with flat refusal, and later with extreme reluctance.

In Jesus' disciples, we see men who are hand-picked by Jesus from their ordinary lives, who struggle with what is being asked of them. Repeatedly, he rebukes them for their lack of faith (Matthew 6: 30; 8: 26; 14: 31; 16: 8). They bicker about their positions in his kingdom, Peter denied him, and they all abandoned him, yet he sends them into the world as the bearers of his word.

And this is the point.

> *We have this treasure in earthen vessels, so that the excellence of the power may be of God and not of us.*
>
> *(2 Corinthians 4: 7)*

Our earthen vessels are not supposed to be like Ming vases or delicate Wedgwood teacups. They are just as likely to be like something manufactured by Armitage Shanks.

God has included us in the dynamic of the Godhead! The Father sends the Son and the Son sends us. We don't feel worthy or able to do this. We can often point to a list of our disqualifications from being used by God but – as we've just seen – we're in good company. Often our disqualifications are the very qualifications that God is looking for. It has been said: *God does not call the qualified; he qualifies the called*.

He does this precisely because we are broken. At the beginning of Chapter 11, I quoted George Herbert's poem on 'Prayer':

> *Lord, how can man preach thy eternal word?*
>   *He is a brittle crazy glass:*
> *Yet in thy temple thou dost him afford*
>   *This glorious and transcendent place,*
>   *To be a window, through thy grace.*

It is because we are 'brittle' and 'crazy' (that is, cracked) that his glory is seen in us. The apostle Paul says this:

> *Therefore most gladly I will rather boast in my infirmities, that the power of Christ may rest upon me.*
>
> *(2 Corinthians 12: 9)*

In Scripture, God only and always sends messengers with a word – of warning, encouragement, salvation or instruction. In the New Testament, however, we also see that part of the apostolic ministry is to support the material needs of the church (for example in Acts 6: 1-7, 1 Corinthians 16: 1-4 and 2 Corinthians 8: 1-7).

Much of the work that churches do today is 'social' in its reach, catering to the material, medical and educational needs of people – and there is a long tradition of this in the Western churches. These things are a legitimate concern for God's people and necessary in our communities (the world would be a much poorer place without the schools, hospitals and other social interventions established by the church over the years), but we must recognise that he sends us to preach the gospel and to make disciples. Regardless of whatever else it achieves, God's 'sending' will always accomplish that. Jesus was often 'moved with compassion' for the people around him, yet the miracles he performed – referred to as signs and wonders – are demonstrations of his God-hood.

What does it mean to be sent?
Growing up in an Evangelical Christian community, when we talked of 'mission' it was a particular thing. It was going overseas (that is, into 'all the world') to preach the gospel to non-believers. To this end, it was allowable to work in a technical capacity as medical staff, as engineers or agricultural consultants. Our heroes were those hardy souls who went out to the back of beyond and built churches out of mud-bricks, or those who translated the Bible into new languages.

Certainly, in my perception, and – I think it's fair to say – in the minds of the people concerned, there was no great sophistication about this. It was a time (in the early 1960s) when classroom walls still had maps of the world with large areas in red, denoting the British Empire. This kind of thinking was already well out of date by then, of course, and well-consigned to history, but shreds of it – a cultural colonialism – lingered among the churches. It still lingers. We were well-intentioned, for the most part, but naïve.

Meanwhile, during this time, the church almost universally slid into a kind of liberal complacency. Britain was a 'Christian country'; no-one was in any particular need – at least not that wouldn't be addressed by the welfare state and the NHS. If there was any analysis of this, it was that if people were Christians, they were unlikely to be Communists.

Times have changed, but some churches still like to do mission by proxy. They will enthusiastically support those working overseas in far-flung locations and carefully follow their exploits. The ardour with which they do this seems to increase as the distance from home increases, but the effect they have in their own town and among their own people is small.

This is not down to laziness or a lack of genuine commitment, but a lack of understanding. They see 'mission' as something that you have to 'go away' to do. *Go into all the world* inevitably means 'all the other places'.

Perhaps that is an unfair caricature and of course it is right to support brothers and sisters elsewhere in the world, especially in places where they are persecuted. But historically, Evangelicals have placed a high value on overseas missions and sometimes haven't identified the very obvious needs at home. We might think that 'Mission' and 'evangelism' should be undertaken by a special corps of crack spiritual troops – 'best left to the Professionals'! We have a low estimation of God's ability or inclination to use us to reach the lost. We think: *who are we to do that?*

But in this we fail to understand that 'mission' is the context of our being here at all. We were sent here! God has planted us here, and in this place he 'pleads through us' (2 Corinthians 5: 20).

Glen Scrivener[21] writes:

> *[Mission] is not a function that we resolve to undertake … it is the very nature of our life together.*

As we have said repeatedly, mission is the natural outcome, the product, of our worship.

Our 'being sent' therefore is the basic purpose of everything we do. As local churches, our purpose is 'to share the love of God and His Gospel' wherever we happen to be.

Our Motivation

It's very easy to talk about 'the world' and 'mankind' as if they are abstracts. 'God so loved *the world…*' But we are talking about people we know: the man next door; the antisocial family down the road; the dysfunctional people … *those who labour and are heavy laden* (Matthew 11: 28) as well as those who think they're fine. We need to put faces and names to these general terms if we are to engage with 'the world'. We must identify with them. Whom are we sent to? People like us – they are broken; we're broken too. God's grace is over us all. As the Apostle Paul says:

> *Blessed be the God and Father of our Lord Jesus Christ, the Father of mercies and God of all comfort,* [4] *who comforts us in all our tribulation, that we may be able to comfort those who are in any trouble, with the comfort with which we ourselves are comforted by God.*

(2 Corinthians 1: 3, 4)

Our brokenness is the key to someone else's healing.

Also, it's easy to fall into the trap of doing good things out of duty or routine. God is motivated by *love* (Ephesians 2: 4ff), so must we be. The love of Christ compels us (2 Corinthians 5: 14). Jesus was moved with compassion: so must we be. We are the vehicle of God's love towards our neighbours, work colleagues and those we meet; God sends us because He is the fountain of sending love.

Sent for what?

God sends us to be salt and light in our homes, our communities and our workplaces. We should expect our mission field to begin close to home.

We are sent to make disciples

Jesus commissions us to *make disciples*, but how? We might think of attendance at a Sunday school or a twelve-week Bible study course. Or maybe a training programme like those offered by YWAM.

But in Scripture, Jesus offers us a model of discipleship in his relationship with his disciples. Several points are worth making.

> *And He went up on the mountain and called to Him those He Himself wanted. And they came to Him. [14] Then He appointed twelve, that they might be with Him and that He might send them out to preach, [15] and to have power to heal sicknesses and to cast out demons.*

(Mark 3: 13-15)

A lot of people were following Jesus, some closely, others from a distance, but Jesus picked these men out for himself. They are a very mixed group and it's hard to tell what his criteria were – certainly not the greatness of their faith or the depth of their understanding. So, the first point about making disciples for Jesus is that he makes the selection.

Jesus called the Twelve to follow him in Mark 3, and in Mark 6 he sent them out on their first mission. In the intervening period he involved them in his teaching and his work, instructing them, directing them, being a model for them and challenging their pre-conceptions and prejudices. The word used here for 'disciple' can also mean 'student'.

After they had returned from their first mission, he took them aside for some much-needed R and R and a debrief ... that turned into the Feeding of the Five Thousand, where they themselves were the means of delivery for Jesus' power.

They do not seem ideal candidates in some ways. Most if not all of them at one time or another showed difficult behaviour or attitudes, or dullness of faith or understanding – and Judas eventually betrayed him to those who wanted him dead. If Jesus had been anyone other than the Lord of Life, his discipling relationship with these men would have ended on the cross.

Making disciples is a big deal. It is not a task to be taken lightly and it will involve our focus and commitment. So, we have to think carefully about what we're doing – and we have to model that discipleship ourselves.

Finally, Jesus called his disciples to be *fishers of men* (Matthew 4: 19). His intention was to make his disciples disciplers. They are the ones that he first told to 'Go…'. We put much emphasis on people 'becoming Christians' and on a momentary decision, but this is not a Scriptural emphasis. The work of being a disciple, of making disciples and of making disciplers is a day-by-day spiritual journey in which we learn how to trust Jesus Christ and walk with him by faith.

What this looks like in practice is a radical Christian lifestyle – one that is constantly aware of its roots and purpose – where we live in accountability to one another in the Body of Christ, where worship is our first language.

We are sent to proclaim

We are sent to proclaim the good news of Jesus Christ. *Jesus appointed twelve, that they might be with Him and that He might send them out to preach* (Mark 3: 14). The first role of a disciple of Jesus Christ is to preach – to declare his word. Paul says:

> *I am not ashamed of this Good News about Christ. It is the power of God at work, saving everyone who believes … This Good News tells us how God makes us right in his sight. This is accomplished from start to finish by faith. As the Scriptures say, "It is through faith that a righteous person has life."*

(Romans 1: 16, 17 NLT)

Without this gospel, there would be no point in making disciples. Jesus and his disciples come together about this message; Jesus is the Word of God made flesh.

This message is good news! *Jesus* is good news! He's the news the world has been waiting for: God's love towards us is so great that he sent his own Son to embrace the consequences of sin and make us free from the curse of the fall. Jesus' death abolishes death (2 Timothy 1: 10) and releases all those who are captive to the fear of death (Hebrews 2: 15).

The simple declaration of his message saves people. When they hear the gospel for the first time and embrace it, they meet Jesus himself – because he is the message.

> *… that you may believe that Jesus is the Christ, the Son of God, and that believing you may have life in His name.*
>
> *(John 20: 31)*
>
> *In [Jesus Christ] you also trusted, after you heard the word of truth, the gospel of your salvation; in whom also, having believed, you were sealed with the Holy Spirit of promise.*
>
> *(Ephesians 1: 13)*

It is this encounter with Jesus Christ, the living Word of God, who submitted himself to death and then rose again that transforms people's lives and turns lost sinners into men and women of God. Only he can accomplish this – no amount of persuading on our part will do it.

Finally, as Jesus said:

> *This is the work of God, that you believe in Him whom He sent.*
>
> (John 6: 29)

The message of Jesus is the grace of God. It is complete in itself. There is nothing we can add to it. As we have reiterated in this book, when God speaks, the only legitimate response is to say 'yes' by faith.

> *Today, if you will hear His voice, do not harden your hearts.*

We are sent to do

Sent to do what?

First let me state for the record that there is nothing we can *do* that will impress God in the least. He is not interested in our religious observance, our charitable deeds, our scintillating career or our skill on the keyboard. This is the kind of thing that Paul calls dung (to put it delicately) when we try to place them before God (Philippians 3: 8). Nevertheless, the Book of James gives us some vital but often misunderstood teaching on the relationship between *faith* and *works*.

While God isn't interested in our works it's likely that our neighbours are.

> *What does it profit, my brethren, if someone says he has faith but does not have works? Can faith*

> *save him? ¹⁵ If a brother or sister is naked and destitute of daily food, ¹⁶ and one of you says to them, "Depart in peace, be warmed and filled," but you do not give them the things which are needed for the body, what does it profit? ¹⁷ Thus also faith by itself, if it does not have works, is dead.*

(James 2: 14-17)

At first glance, this appears to contradict what Paul says in Romans about 'Justification by Faith', but it doesn't. Real faith produces fruit. It has an output.

It's no good going up to a homeless person and giving them an encouraging scripture, or even telling them about Jesus, unless we are at least prepared to do something about his homelessness. This would be empty and hypocritical, and is almost exactly what the Pharisees were doing in Mark 7:

> *[Jesus] said to them, "All too well you reject the commandment of God, that you may keep your tradition. ¹⁰ For Moses said, 'Honour your father and your mother' … ¹¹ But you say, 'If a man says to his father or mother, "Whatever profit you might have received from me is Corban"—' (that is, a gift to God), ¹² then you no longer let him do anything for his father or his mother, ¹³ making the word of God of no effect through your tradition which you have handed down."*

(Mark 7: 9-13)

They found ways to avoid keeping their God-ordained duty to their parents by pretending that they had a higher responsibility.

Jesus tells us to *love our neighbour as ourselves* (Matthew 22: 39), so if we intend to share the gospel with a person living on the street with a view to making him or her a disciple of Jesus Christ, we will probably find it necessary to do something practical to help him first, otherwise our words will mean nothing to him.

That's obvious really, but it means that if we are serious about proclaiming the word of Christ and making disciples to him, these things have to be accompanied by appropriate works of righteousness.

Summary

Mission is a necessary response to worship.

In our previous study of Psalm 95 we saw that there are three movements in worship:

Oh come, let us sing unto the LORD (v.1)

Oh come, let us worship and bow down (v.6), and

Today, if you will hear His voice, do not harden your hearts... (vv.7, 8)

These three movements correspond to the zones of the tabernacle; the Outer Court, the Holy Place and the Most Holy Place, where we meet with God in person. In attitudes of worship, God's people encounter him and hear his voice. He calls us to respond and then says 'Go'. We examined this in Isaiah 6 and Matthew 28.

God's command to 'Go' results in us being commissioned or 'sent' to serve him. I believe that we should expect to hear God speaking to us and either commissioning us for service or reiterating that commission each time we worship – which is to say that we should live our lives in a constant awareness and recognition of his call.

Mission is an essential aspect of God himself.

As the Father sends the Son; the Father and the Son send the Holy Spirit and the Son sends us, we (as Christ's Body) are incorporated into the dynamic of the Godhead in a way that is impossible to comprehend fully.

When a person is sent, they speak and act with the authority of the sender – so Jesus says:

> *I can of Myself do nothing. As I hear, I judge; and My judgment is righteous, because I do not seek My own will but the will of the Father who sent Me.*
>
> *(John 5: 30)*

Paul's authority to preach came from his encounter with Jesus on the road to Damascus (Acts 22: 10) and he is often at pains to point out his apostleship (for example in Romans 1: 1). Although for practical purposes, we might find ourselves part of a church ministry and acting at the direction of its leadership, ultimately our authority to make disciples, proclaim the word of God or to do righteous acts must come from the same place as Paul's.

Although our own ministries and our God-given visions are quite distinct, they all arise in the presence of God, in our times of intimacy with him. This is a wonderful thing because it means that God himself, through the Holy Spirit, is directly involved in the decisions and activities of his people.

Mission must be in line with the Word of God

What God says to you while you're in his presence is a unique thing to you. It flows from your relationship with him. In all likelihood, what God is saying to you in private will accord with what he's saying to others around you, who will recognise your calling – including the leadership of the churches we belong to. God always moves in an orderly way.

Your 'sending' will be unique to you, however God will not contradict his word. God's sending will have these characteristics:

- It will promote making disciples to Jesus Christ (Matthew 28: 19).
- It will be based on proclaiming the gospel of Jesus Christ (Mark 16: 15; Romans 1: 16).
- It will usually involve works of righteousness that support the other two.

God's mission will also promote unity and strength in the church, and it will always glorify the name of Jesus. As the natural outflow of worship, it will establish a space where God is worshipped and where God's kingdom, at least in part, can be enjoyed on earth.

Discussion 14

What is your understanding of 'mission'?

Do you consider that you have a mission?

How can worship lead directly to mission?

Have you ever struggled to share your faith?

When leading worship, there is considerable danger that we can become contaminated by worldly thinking.

- Give some examples of this contamination.
- How might these be avoided?

In worship, there should be an opportunity to respond to what the Holy Spirit is saying.

- How can you create space for people to respond to what God is saying?

Take two different examples of worship acts, for example: a Church of England morning service, a worship session streamed on YouTube, or a service at your own church:

- Can you see a structure or 'journey' through the worship? Where did it take you?
- Are there opportunities for the congregation to respond to what God might be saying?

- Are there opportunities for congregational participation?
- Are there opportunities for spiritual gifts to be used in line with Paul's teaching (Romans 12; 1 Cor 12 and 14)?

Bibliography

Select Bibliography

Allison, S. M. (2002). *God is Building a House*. London: John Hunt Publishing.

Clift, S., & Hancox, G. (2001). *The Perceived Benefits of Singing*: findings from preliminary surveys with a university college choral society. Journal for the Royal Society for the Promotion of Health.

Ellis, C. J. (2009). *Approaching God*: A guide for worship leaders and worshippers. Norwich: Canterbury Press.

Kauflin, B. (2008). *Worship Matters*. Wheaton, Illinois: Crossway Books.

Kreutz, G. (2003). Does Singing Provide Health Benefits? Proceedings of the 5th Triennial ESCOM Conference, (pp. 216-219).

Scofield, C. (1909). *The Annotated Bible*. Oxford: OUP.

Stacey, R., & Brittain, K. (2002). *Singing for Health*: an exploration of the issues. Health Education, 102(4), 156-162.

Wommack, A. (2007). *Grace, The Power of the Gospel*. Walsall: Andrew Wommack Ministries, Europe.

Wommack, A. (2008). *The War is Over*. Tulsa: Harrison House Publishers.

Other Notes and References

Giglio, Louie (2008) Indescribable, DVD, Sparrow Records.

Kazenske, Donna, retrieved from http://sureword.faithweb.com/wordofknowledge.html.

Tozer, A.W. (1976, 2008) *The Knowledge of the Holy*, Milton Keynes, Authentic Media.

Tim Hughes and **Al Gordon** (2011), Worship Central Course.

Philip Yancey, 'Holy Sex' in Christianity Today, October 1, 2003.

End Notes

1 Louie Giglio, Indescribable, 2008, DVD, Sparrow Records.

2 Liturgy: the word comes from two Greek words: *leitos*, meaning 'public' and *ergos*, meaning 'an action', and means 'What we do together'.

3 Kauflin (2008)

4   Particularly good on the character and qualities of worship leaders and the dynamic of worship teams are: Kauflin, 2008 (ibid), and the Worship Central Course by Tim Hughes and Al Gordon (2011) available at WorshipCentral.org.

5   Sometimes, other people could go into the Tabernacle with the priest, for example to perform a vow (Numbers 6: 1-21).

6   There's no Biblical record of this happening in the Tabernacle, although some of the Psalms imply it, but it certainly did at Solomon's Temple. For us, song is an important feature of worship.

7   1 Kings 6: 29-35 describes the interior decoration of Solomon's Temple.

8   The image intended here is of a military encampment with colourful tents and banners spread out across the valley with the LORD of Hosts (Yahweh Sabaoth) at its head.

9   I credit three things—classical music, the beauty of nature, and romantic love—as responsible for my own conversion, Philip Yancey, 'Holy Sex' in Christianity Today, October 1, 2003, online at http://www.ctlibrary.com/ct/2003/october/3.46.html, accessed 12 March 2013.

10   Allison, S. M. (2002).

11   'Devil' and 'Satan' both mean accuser. In Classical Greek legal documents, the diabolos (from which we get 'devil') was the prosecuting counsel. Diabolos comes from two words: dia meaning across, and bolos meaning a strike or a throw; it literally means 'one who throws across'. In the Greek law courts, his role was to accuse and to challenge the testimony of a defendant. This is exactly what Satan does to us.

12   Open prayer: When a person prays aloud in the congregation in a regular worship meeting, that person is leading the church in prayer, not praying privately. This is not always well understood, especially if the prayer is unprepared and 'spontaneous'. Therefore, he or she must speak loud enough for everyone to hear and be reasonably brief, or others will not be able to follow them. There is a saying: stand up, speak up and shut up.

13   Acts 6: 8; Acts 8: 6–7; Acts 9: 17–19; Acts 10: 44–46, and Acts 19: 6–7.

14   Donna Kazenske, retrieved from http://sureword.faithweb.com/wordofknowledge.html, accessed 31st Jan 2013.

15 *Agapë* is almost the only Greek word used for 'love' in the New Testament. It stands for self-sacrificial love; the love of Christ.

16 The best translation seems to be 'anointing oil', though the word is different from the one used elsewhere in the Old Testament. Most modern translations seem to struggle to make sense of it: The New King James seems clearest. It is the promise of God in the Law, the people's obedience and specifically Hezekiah's faith that will break the Assyrian strangle-hold.

17 Begotten: an old-fashioned word meaning procreated or generated. In other words, God is physically his Father.

18 Donald Rumsfeld, former U.S. Secretary of Defense and accidental poet said: There are known knowns; there are things we know we know. We also know there are known unknowns; that is to say, we know there are some things we do not know. But there are also unknown unknowns – the ones we don't know we don't know.

19 Sisters in Christ are still 'sons' in the same way that brothers in Christ are in the Bride. It's to do with relationships, not gender. They are also kings, not queens!

20 Remember that in Bible times, only sons could usually inherit.

21 Glen Scrivener at Theology Network: http://www.theologynetwork.org/theology-of-everything/mission-and-evangelism-1.htm

Printed in Great Britain
by Amazon